RATAN TATA

A SUCCESS STORY

RAMPRAKASH SINGH PAVAIYA

TRUE SIGN
PUBLISHING HOUSE

Published by True Sign Publishing House
Address: SY. No. 21/2 & 21/3, Sonnenahalli,
Krishnarajapura, Bengaluru,
Karnataka - 560049 India
E-mail: truesignbooks@gmail.com
Website: www.truesign.in

Ratan Tata: A Success Story

Author: Ramprakash Singh Pavaiya

ISBN: 978-93-5904-721-8

First Edition: 2023

CONTENTS

Introduction

Ratan Tata is a well-known industrialist, investor and retired chairman of Tata Sons in India. Ratan Tata was the chairman of Mishra Tata Group from 1991 to 2012. He left his Tata Group chairmanship on 28th December 2012, but Ratan Tata continues to be the chairman of the "Tata Group" charitable trust.

He is famous all over the world for making the world's smallest car. He took the Tata Group to a new height on the strength of his intelligence and ability. Ratan Tataji as the chairman of Tata Group has also illuminated the name of Tata Group in the country and abroad.

Ratan Tata is a well-known industrialist as well as a noble person, who is also known for his generosity. He always helps the helpless, poor and the needy.

In the year 2020, he has also donated a large amount to help people infected with coronavirus (COVID-19). He is counted among the richest people in the world, so let's know more about him.

Birth and Family

Before knowing about Ratanji Bhai Tata, let's take a look at his family and family history. I hope that this biography will be more interesting and pleasing.

Jamsetji Tata, the head of the Tata family was born to Nusserwanji and Jeevanbai Tata on 3rd March, 1839 in Navsari, a city in southern Gujarat. Tata married Hirabai Daboo. His sons, Dorabji Tata and Ratanji Tata, succeeded Tata as the chairman of the Tata Group. Tata's first cousin was Ratanji Dadabhai Tata, who was instrumental in the founding of the Tata Group. His family was part of a minority group of Parsis who came to India after fleeing persecution of the Parsis in Iran. He was born in the family of a respected but poor priest. His father Nusserwanji was the first businessman in a family of Parsi priests. His mother tongue was Gujarati. He broke with his family's priestly tradition to become the first member of the family to start a business. He started an export trading firm in Mumbai.

Unlike other Parsi people, Jamsetji Tata received formal Western education as his parents observed that he was gifted with special mental arithmetic from an early age. However, he was later sent to Bombay to get a more modern education. He joined his father, Nusserwanji in Bombay at the age of 14 and joined Elphinstone College to complete his education as a "Green Scholar" (equivalent to graduation). He was married in his studenthood, his wife's name was Hirabai Daboo.

After graduating from Bombay's Elphinstone College in 1858, he joined his father's export-trading firm, and helped establish its strong branches in Japan, China, Europe and the United States. It was a turbulent or rather difficult time to start a business as the Indian Rebellion of 1857 was suppressed by the British Government. Nusserwanji Tata regularly traveled to China to get acquainted with the opium trade. It is here that the Parsis are believed to have acquired a taste for opium trade. This prompted the British to expand the market for opium in China.

Nusserwanji Tata wanted his son to be a part of this business, so he sent him to China to learn the details about the opium trade there. However, when Tata traveled to China, he began to realize that the cotton industry was booming and there was a chance to make a huge profit.

Tata worked in his father's company till the age of 29. He founded a trading company in 1868 with a capital of ₹21,000 (US$52 million in 2015 prices). He bought a bankrupt oil mill at Chinchpokli in 1869 and converted it into a cotton mill, which he named Alexandra Mill. He sold the mill after 2 years for profit. Later, in 1874, Jamsetji Tata established the Central India Spinning, Weaving and Manufacturing Company in Nagpur as it seemed like a suitable place for him to set up another business venture. Due to this unconventional location, the people of Bombay scorned the Tatas for not taking smart steps by moving the cotton business in Bombay, known as the "Cottonpolis" of India. He did not understand why he went to the undeveloped city of Nagpur to start a new business.

However, Tata's selection of Nagpur brought him success. Unlike Bombay, land in Nagpur was cheap and readily available for resources. There was abundant agricultural produce, distribution was easy, and cheap land later converted the railway to Nagpur, which further developed the city. Shortly after, in 1877, the Tatas established a new cotton mill, the "Empress Mill", when Queen Victoria was proclaimed Empress of India on 1st January, 1877.

He had four goals in life:

1. Establishment of Iron and Steel Company

2. World Class Educational Institutions

3. Unique Hotel (Taj Hotel, Mumbai)

4. Hydroelectric Plants

The only hotel in his lifetime became a reality with the opening of the Taj Mahal hotel at Colaba waterfront in Mumbai at a cost of ₹11 million (₹11 billion in 2015 prices) on 3rd December, 1903. At that time it was the only hotel in India that had electricity.

In 1885, Tata started another company in Pondicherry, with the sole purpose of distributing Indian textiles to the nearby French colonies and not paying a fee; However, it failed due to insufficient demand for clothing.

It purchased Dharmasi Mills in Kurla in Bombay and later resold it to purchase Advance Mills in Ahmedabad. Tata named it Advance Mills as it was one of the most hi-tech mills of that time. On top of its technology, the company left a major impact on the city of Ahmedabad as the Tatas attempted to integrate the mill within the city to provide economic development to their community. Through these many contributions, Tatas furthered the textile and cotton industry in India. Jamsetji Tata remained an important figure in the industrial world even in the later stages of his life. Later, Tata became a strong supporter of indigenousism.

The **Swadeshi Movement** did not start until 1905;. However, Tata represented these same principles during his lifetime. Swadeshi was a political movement in British India that encouraged the production of domestic goods and the boycott of imported goods. Impressed by its principles, Tata named his new cotton mill at Bombay as "Swadeshi Mill". The original purpose of this new mill was to produce fine cloth like the one coming from Manchester. Manchester was famous for the production of soft cloth, and the coarse cloth produced in India was no longer being liked by the public.

The Tatas wanted to produce fabric of higher quality than Manchester cloth in an effort to reduce the number of imports coming from abroad. He had a far-reaching vision of becoming the primary manufacturer of all types of clothing for India and eventually becoming an exporter. They wanted India to be the only producer of the fine fabrics for which the primitive weavers of India were famous. The Tatas began experimenting with various methods to improve the cultivation of cotton grown in different parts of India. He believed that by adopting the method of cultivation used by the Egyptian ryots (farmers), who were famous for their soft cotton, they always strived to help India's cotton industry reach these goals. Tata had introduced ring spindles in their mills, which soon replaced the throttles that were once used by manufacturers.

The work of his successors received three remaining ideas:

- **Tata Steel** (formerly TISCO - Tata Iron and Steel Company Limited) is Asia's first and India's largest steel company. It became the fifth largest steel company in the world after it acquired Corus Group, which produces 28 million tonnes of steel annually.

- **The Indian Institute of Science**, Bangalore, is a premier Indian institute for research and education in science and engineering.

- **Tata Hydroelectric Power Supply Company** renamed as Tata Power Company Limited, which is currently the largest private power company in India with an installed generation capacity of over 8000MW.

Jamsetji donated generously mainly for education and healthcare. He was named as the greatest philanthropist of the last century by the **EdelGive Foundation and Hurun Research India.** He has topped the list of the world's top philanthropists of the 20th century, with an estimated donation of $102 billion, adjusted for inflation.

During a business trip to Germany in 1900, Tata became seriously ill. .He died in Bad Nauheim on 19th May 1904, and was buried in the Parsi burial ground in Brookwood Cemetery, Woking, England.

Tata's Iron and Steel plant was established at Sakchi village in Jharkhand. The village developed into a town and the railway station there was named Tatanagar. Now, it is a bustling metropolis known as Jamshedpur in Jharkhand, named in his honour. The old village of Sakchi (now urbanised) now exists within the city of Jamshedpur. Tata became a founding member of the Tata family.

Jamsetji Nusserwanji Tata was an Indian leading industrialist who founded the Tata Group, India's largest conglomerate company. Named by many polls and ranking lists as the greatest philanthropist of the last century, he also founded the city of Jamshedpur.

Jamsetji Tata is considered the great "Father of Indian Industry." He was so influential in the industry that Jawaharlal Nehru referred to the Tatas as the One-Man Planning Commission. Tata, a businessman in his early life, changed the business world of India through his many ventures within the cotton and cast iron industry, and is known as one of the most important builders of the modern Indian economy. . Among his many achievements, Tata Iron and Steel Works Company in Tata Jamshedpur is particularly notable.

Jamsetji Tata had two sons Ratanji Tata and Dorabji Tata. Ratanji Tata was born in Bombay in British India as the son of the famous Parsi businessman Jamsetji Tata. Ratan Tata was educated at St. Xavier's College in Bombay and later joined his father's firm. Upon Jamsetji Tata's death in 1904, Ratan Tata and his brother Dorabji Tata inherited a large estate, much of which they devoted to philanthropic works of a practical nature and the establishment of various industrial enterprises for the development of India's resources .

The **Indian Institute of Scientific and Medical Research** (Indian Institute of Science, IISc) was established in Bangalore in 1905, and in 1912 Tata Steel began operations at Sakchi in the Central Provinces with remarkable success. However, the most important of the Tata enterprises was the hydropower storage of the Western Ghats (1915), which provided Bombay with enormous amounts of electric power, and therefore greatly increased the productive capacity of its industries.

Sir Ratan Tata, who was knighted in 1916, did not limit his favors to India. In England, where he had a permanent residence at York House, Twickenham, he established the Ratan Tata Department of Social Sciences and Administration at the London School of Economics in 1912, and the Ratan Tata Fund at the University of London to study conditions of the poor. In 1909, he donated an amount of Rs. 50,000 (equivalent to about 40 million rupees in 2022) to Mahatma Gandhi in the struggle for the right of Indians to work in the Transvaal. This donation helped secure the finances of Gandhi's protest against the Anglo-Boer rulers.

He was a great connoisseur of art. The **Chhatrapati Shivaji Maharaj Vastu Sangrahalaya** (formerly the Prince of Wales Museum) has a section displaying the collections of Sir Ratanji Tata (acquired in 1923), as well as those of Sir Dorab Tata (acquired in 1933) and Sir Purushottam Mavji (acquired in 1933). There are two other sections.

He married Navajbai Sett in 1893 and moved to England for the last time in 1915. He adopted Naval Tata from the family of a distant relative. He died on 5th September 1918 at St Ives in Cornwall, England and was buried by his father (Jamsetji Tata) at Brookwood Cemetery, Woking, near London.

Sir Dorabji Tata (27th August 1859 – 3rd June 1932), the second son of Jamsetji Tata, was an Indian businessman from the British Raj, and a key figure in the history and development of the Tata Group. He was knighted in 1910 for his contribution to industry in British India. Tata received his primary education at the Proprietary High School in Bombay (now Mumbai) before moving to England in 1875, where he was taught privately. He joined Gonville and Caius College, Cambridge in 1877, where he stayed for two years before returning to Bombay in 1879. He continued his studies at St. Xavier's College, Bombay, where he obtained a degree in 1882.

Upon graduation, Dorab worked for two years as a journalist in the Bombay Gazette. In 1884, he joined the cotton business department of his father's firm. He was sent first to Pondicherry, then a French colony, to determine whether a cotton mill could be profitable there. Thereafter, he was sent to Nagpur to learn the cotton trade at the Empress Mills established by his father in 1877.

Dorabji's father, Jamsetji, had visited Mysore state in South India for business purposes, where he met Dr. Hormusji Bhabha, a Parsi and the first Indian Inspector General of Education of that state. While visiting Bhabha's house, there he met Bhabha's only daughter, young Meherbai and took her for his son. Returning to Bombay, Jamsetji sent Dorabji to the kingdom of Mysore, specifically to summon the Bhabha family. Dorab did the same and duly married Meherbai in 1897. The couple had no children. Meherbai's brother, Jehangir Bhabha, became a reputed lawyer. He was the father of scientist Homi J. Bhabha. Thus Dorabji was Homi Bhabha's uncle by marriage. The Tata Group funded Bhabha's research and his research institutions, including the **Tata Institute of Fundamental Research.**

Dorabji was deeply involved in the realization of his father's ideas of a modern iron and steel industry, and agreed on the need for hydroelectric power to power the industry. Dorab is credited with founding the **Tata Steel** Group in 1907, which was founded by his father, and **Tata Power** in 1911, the core of the present-day Tata Group.

Dorabji was also with the mineralogists who discovered the iron mines. His presence is said to have encouraged researchers to explore areas that were otherwise neglected. Under Dorabji's management, the business that once included three cotton mills and the Taj Hotel Bombay grew into India's largest private sector steel company, three electric companies and one of India's leading insurance companies. He was the founder of the **New India Assurance Company Limited** in 1919, India's largest general insurance company. Dorabji Tata was knighted as Sir Dorabji Tata by Edward VII in January 1910.

Dorabji was extremely fond of sports, and a pioneer in the Indian Olympic movement. As President of the Indian Olympic Association, he financed the Indian contingent for the Paris Olympics in 1924. The Tata family, like most of India's big businessmen, were Indian nationalists.

Tata was also a member of the International Olympic Committee during most of the years between World War I and World War II.

Meherbai Tata died of leukemia in 1931 at the age of 52. Shortly after her death, Dorabji established the **Lady Tata Memorial Trust** to further the study of diseases of the blood. Dorabji died at the age of 73 on 3rd June 1932 in Bad Kissingen, Germany. He is buried with his wife Meherbai at Brookwood Cemetery, Woking, England.

Dorabji Tata had no children but Sir Ratanji Tata had an adopted son, Navalji Tata. Navalji Tata was born on 30th August 1904 in Surat in a middle class family. His father was working as a spinning master in Advanced Mills in Ahmedabad. After his death in 1908, his family shifted to Navsari. The young Naval, who earned some income from his mother's embroidery work, was later sent by family friends to the **JN Petit Parsee Orphanage** to help them. A fateful turn of life changed Naval's fortunes and life, Ratanji Tata's wife, Lady Navajbai Tata adopted him from the orphanage. Naval was 13 when he was adopted by Lady Tata. Naval Tata later graduated in economics from Bombay University and went to London for a short course in accounting.

Naval's first wife was Sooni Commissariat; they had two sons, Ratan and Jimmy. The couple separated in the mid-1940s. Naval later married Simone Dunoyer, a businesswoman from Switzerland, they got married in 1955. Noel Tata is their son.

In 1930, he joined Tata Sons as a dispatch clerk-cum-assistant secretary and soon became the assistant secretary of Tata Sons Ltd. In 1933, he became the Secretary of the Department of Aviation and five years later, he joined the Department of Textiles as an executive. In 1939 he became the joint managing director of Tata Mills - the controlling company of textile mills run by the Tatas, and in 1947 became its managing director. On 1st February 1941, he became the director of Tata Sons. He took over as the Managing Director of Tata Oil Mills Company Limited in 1948. He was also the chairman of Ahmedabad Advance Mills, a Tata Group company based in Ahmedabad.

Over the years he became president of other textile mills and three electric companies. From an active director, he later became the Vice President of Tata Sons. He was directly responsible for the management of three Tata electric companies, four textile mills and the Sir Ratan Tata Trust. He was the longest-serving aide on the board of Tata Sons and a close associate of JRD Tata. He died on 5th May, 1989 in Bombay due to cancer.

Now, we move on to the aspect related to his biography. Ratan Tata was born on 28th December, 1937 in Bombay, now Mumbai, during the British Raj, and is the son of Naval Tata (born in Surat). His grandmother was the sister of Hirabai Tata, wife of Tata Group founder Jamsetji Tata. His grandfather, Hormusji Tata, was a relative of the Tata family, so Ratan was a Tata by birth. Parents Naval and Sooni separated in 1948 when Ratan was 10-years-old, and he was later raised by Sir Ratanji Tata's widow and his grandmother Navajbai Tata who formally moved his father Naval Tata to the JN Petit Parsee Orphanage. He has a half-brother, Noel Tata (from Naval Tata's second marriage to Simone Tata), with whom he was raised.

He attended Campion School, Mumbai until 8th grade, then at Cathedral and John Connon School, Mumbai and Bishop Cotton School in Shimla [and graduated from Riverdale Country School in New York City in 1955]. In 1959, he received a degree in architecture from Cornell University, and in 1975, attended Harvard Business School's seven-week advanced management program. Promoted to management during the 1970s, Ratan brought all-around early success to the group company **National Radio and Electronics** (NELCO), which was on the verge of bankruptcy during an economic downturn. In 1991, JRD stepped down as chairman of Tata Sons, he was named the next successor. When he moved to the new role, he faced stiff resistance from the heads of several companies, some of whom had spent decades in their respective companies and became very powerful and influential because of the freedom to operate under JRD Tata. He began to change them by setting a retirement age, and then reporting operations to the group office to individual companies, each contributing some of their profits to building and using the Tata Group's brand. Innovation was given priority and young talent was inducted and given responsibilities. Under his leadership, the operations of the group companies were streamlined as a whole.

During the 21 years he led the Tata Group, growing revenue 40 times and profits more than 50 times. When he took over, the Tata Group as a whole was largely sold by goods, and when he left, most of the sales came from brands. He boldly got **Tata Tea** to acquire **Tetley**, **Tata Motors** to acquire **Jaguar Land Rover** and **Tata Steel** to acquire **Corus**. This transformed Tata from a largely India-focused conglomerate into a global business, with over 65% of revenues from operations and sales in over 100 countries. He presented the concept of **Tata Nano car**.

Tata invested personal savings in **Snapdeal**, one of India's leading e-commerce websites, and in January 2016, **Teabox**, an online premium Indian tea seller, and CashKaro.com, a discount coupon and cash-back website. He has made small investments in both early and late stage companies in India, such as Rs 0.95 crore in **Ola cabs**. In April 2015, it was reported that Tata had acquired a stake in Chinese smartphone startup **Xiaomi**. In 2016, he invested in Nestway, an online portal to find fully furnished flats for bachelors, Tata Motors launched the first assignment of Tigor electric vehicles from its Sanand plant in Gujarat. According to Ratan Tata, "Tigor indicates willingness to rapidly pursue India's electric dream. Government sets ambitious target of having electric cars only by 2030."

Education and Career

In the first major phase of Ratan Tata's education, he completed his early schooling from Campion School, Mumbai till 8th standard. Recently, Tata spoke about his childhood days on a Facebook page called "**Humans of Bombay.**" The divorce caused trouble because "it was not as common as it is today". When his mother remarried, the boys in the school began to make many comments, but he encouraged his grandmother to teach him and his brother to maintain "dignity at all costs" and to fight through difficult situations. He learned from his grandmother to learn to fight with such situations and not to run away.

Ratan Tata's secondary and senior secondary education was completed at the Cathedral and John Connon School, Mumbai and then at the Bishop Cotton School in Shimla. He was a brilliant student in his school and college and described in the Facebook Chronicle page, "Humans of Bombay", how his father always suggested the opposite of what he wanted him to do. Like once he asked to play the violin that he wanted to play, so his father asked him to learn the piano. Similarly, when he wanted to go to UK for studies, his father sent him to America.

He always credits his grandmother for encouraging him to pursue his passion for architecture as his father wanted him to become an engineer but he wanted to be an architect. Moving towards higher education, Ratan Tata enrolled for a degree in Mechanical Engineering, but at the insistence of his grandmother, he changed his studies and completed his graduation in Architecture. This decision upset his father but Tata was happy because he was independent and it was his grandmother who constantly taught him "the courage to speak but to be soft and respectful." Later in 1975, he also completed an advanced management program from Harvard Business School in 1975.

Career:

Before returning to India, Ratan briefly worked at **Jones and Emmons** in Los Angeles, California. He started his career with the Tata Group in 1961. In the initial days, he worked on the shop floor of Tata Steel. After this he joined with other companies of Tata Group. In 1971, he was appointed Director-in-Charge in the **National Radio and Electronics Company** (NELCO). In 1981, he was made the chairman of Tata Industries. In 1991, JRD Tata stepped down as the chairman of the group and made Ratan Tata his successor.

The Tata Group scaled new heights under Ratan's leadership. Under his leadership Tata Consultancy Services issued a public issue and Tata Motors was listed on the New York Stock Exchange. In 1998, Tata Motors introduced the first fully Indian passenger car – the **Tata Indica**. Subsequently, Tata Tea acquired 'Tetley', Tata Motors 'Jaguar Land Rover' and Tata Steel acquired 'Corus', which greatly increased the reputation of the Tata Group in the Indian industry. The Tata Nano - the world's cheapest passenger car - is also the result of Ratan Tata's thinking.

He retired from all executive responsibilities of the Tata Group on 28th December 2012. He was replaced by 44-year-old Cyrus Mistry. Although Tata is now retired, he is still engaged in business. More recently, he has made his personal investment in India's e-commerce company Snapdeal. Along with this, he has also invested in another e-commerce company, Urban Ladder and Chinese mobile company, Xiaomi.

Ratan is currently the retired Chairman of the Tata Group. Along with this, he also remains the chairman of two trusts of Tata Sons.

Ratan Tata has played an important role in many organizations in India as well as in other countries. He is a member of the Prime Minister's Council on Trade and Industry and the National Manufacturing Competitiveness Council. Ratan is also a director on the boards of several companies.

Ratan Tata started his career in the Tata Group in 1962. Earlier, he used to handle limestone shovel and blast furnace on the shop floor of Tata Steel. In 1991, JRD Tata stepped down as chairman of Tata Industries and named Ratan Tata as his successor. Under Ratan, Tata Tea acquired Tetley, Tata Motors acquired Jaguar Land Rover and Tata Steel acquired Chorus. These victories transformed Tata from a large India-focused company into a global business, with 65% of its revenues coming from overseas. He also contributed to the development of Indica and Nano.

In 1971, he was appointed as the Director-in-Charge of the National Radio and Electronics Company Limited (NELCO) to help his struggling finances. He worked towards creating a better consumer electronics division but economic slowdown and union strikes prevented him from achieving success.

In 1977, he was transferred to Empress Mills, a struggling textile mill within the Tata Group. He proposed a plan for the mill but other Tata executives rejected it and the mill was closed. Later, he was moved to Tata Industries.

In 1991, JRD Tata appointed him as the new chairman of the Tata Group of Companies. The decision came under scrutiny following objections from other company officials and questions were raised about their ability to run the corporation.

But he was successful in improving the financial success of the industries and under his leadership expanded the growth of the organization. He changed the management and vision of the division, and managed to bring in fairly large dividends.

He also became a member of the Prime Minister's Council on Trade and Industry. He served on the advisory board of **RAND's Centre for Asia-Pacific Policy** and is also an active participant in India's AIDS Initiative program.

He also holds membership of the International Advisory Boards of Mitsubishi Cooperation, American International Group, JP Morgan Chase and Booz Allen Hamilton.

On his 75th birthday, he resigned from the post of Chairman of Tata Group and was replaced by Cyrus Mistry, Managing Director of Shapoorji Pallonji Group. Even after retirement, he is still an active businessman and invests in upcoming promising business ventures

Ratan Tata has also worked in various organizations in India and abroad. He is a member of the Prime Minister's Council on Trade and Industry and is also on the Board of Governors of the East-West Center, an advisory board to RAND's Center for Asia-Pacific Policy. He also serves on the program board of the Bill & Melinda Gates Foundation's.

He was awarded the **Padma Bhushan** by the Government of India in January 2000. He serves on the boards of several major organizations in both the public and private sectors in India. He is a member of the International Investment Council set up by the President of South Africa and serves on the program board of the Bill & Melinda Gates Foundation's. Ratan Tata is credited with Tata's successful bid for Anglo-Dutch steel and aluminum producer Corus, which was acquired by Tata Sons for an estimated $6.7 billion.

He made a comeback in October 2016 replacing Cyrus Mistry. A selection committee has already been formed with the aim of finding a successor in another four months.

Ratanjibhai Tata worked tirelessly from his education till he touched the heights of his career. Today, Tatas are known everywhere in the country and the world in every field, whether it is business or philanthropy, with a different identity.

Business and Companies

The Tata Group

The Tata Group is an Indian multinational conglomerate headquartered in Mumbai. Founded in 1868, it is India's largest conglomerate, with products and services in over 150 countries, and operations in 100 countries across six continents. Acknowledged as the founder of the Tata Group, Jamsetji Tata is sometimes referred to as the "Father of Indian Industry."

The group gained international recognition after acquiring several global companies. Each Tata company operates independently under the guidance and supervision of its own board of directors and shareholders. Charitable trusts control 66% of the Tata holding company Tata Sons, while the Tata family is a much smaller shareholder.

As of 2022, the group had an estimated annual revenue of US$128 billion. In 2018, it contributed about 4 per cent of the country's GDP and paid 2.24% of total taxation in India, the highest by any corporate group.

There are 29 publicly listed Tata Group companies with a combined market capitalization of $311 billion (INR 23.4 trillion) as of December 31st , 2021. Important associates of the Tata Group include Tata Consultancy Services, Tata Consumer Products, Tata Motors, Tata Power, Tata Steel, Voltas, Titan Company, Tanishq, Tata Chemicals, Tata Communications, Trent, Tata Alexei, Indian Hotels Company, Air India, TajAir, Tata Cliq, Tata Capital, Croma and Tata Starbucks.

History of Tata Group

As published in the **Journal of the Royal Society of Arts** on August 27th 1848, The House of Tata by Sir Frederick James, OBE - Sixty Years of Industrial Development in India - "Jamsetji Nusserwanji Tata was born in 1839, just after Macaulay's departure. India went on to write its famous history of England... He graduated from Bombay's Elphinstone College in

1858. Shortly after, he joined his father's trading firm that dealt in general merchandise. There, Junior Tata specialized in developing trade with China.

When the American Civil War caused a boom in the Bombay cotton market, Tata and his father joined the Asian Banking Corporation. When the tide turned low, Tata's credit was ruined. Fortunately, the firm's credit was re-established during the next three years. A share in the lucrative contract for the Commissariat of Napier's expedition to Abyssinia in 1868 restored the family fortune. With a capital of Rs 21,000 in 1870, he founded a trading company. In addition, he established a trading company at Chinchpokli. Bought a bankrupt oil mill and converted it into a cotton mill named Alexandra Mill, which he sold for profit two years later. In 1874, he established another cotton mill in Nagpur named Empress Mill. He achieved four goals set up an iron and steel company, a unique hotel, a world-class educational institution and a hydroelectric plant. During his lifetime, in 1903, the Taj Mahal hotel was opened on the Colaba coast, making it the first in India to have electricity.

1904-1938:

After Jamsetji's death, his eldest son, Dorabji Tata became the chairman in 1904. Sir Dorabji founded the **Tata Iron and Steel Company** (TISCO), now known as Tata Steel, in 1907. marking the group's global ambitions,. Tata Limited opened its first overseas office in London. Following the founder's goals, western India's first hydro plant was brought to life, giving birth to Tata Power. Yet another dream, the **Indian Institute of Science** was established in 1911 with the admission of the first batch.

1938-1991:

JRD Tata was made the chairman of the Tata Group in 1938. Under his chairmanship, the Tata Group's assets grew from US$101 million to over US$5 billion. Starting with 14 enterprises, half a century after his departure in 1988, Tata Sons had grown into a conglomerate of 95 enterprises. These enterprises included enterprises that the company had either started or in which they controlled their interest. New sectors such as chemicals, technology, cosmetics, marketing, engineering, manufacturing, tea and software services brought them recognition.

In 1952, JRD established an airline known as **Tata Air Services** (later renamed Tata Airlines). In 1953, the Government of India passed the Air

Corporation Act and bought a majority stake in the carrier from Tata Sons, although JRD Tata would remain as chairman until 1977.

In 1945, Tata Motors was established, which first focused on engines. In 1954, it entered the commercial vehicle market after forming a joint venture with Daimler-Benz. Tata Consultancy Services was established in 1968.

1991–Present Day:

In 1991, Ratan Tata became the chairman of the Tata Group. It was also the year of economic liberalization in India, which opened the market to foreign competitors. During this time, the Tata Group began acquiring several companies, including Tetley (2000), the Corus Group (2007), and Jaguar and Land Rover (2008).

In 2008, the subsidiary Tata Motors launched the Tata Nano, which they described as "the cheapest car in the world."

In 2017, Natarajan Chandrasekaran was appointed as the chairman. He was instrumental in restructuring business verticals and increasing the ownership of promoter stake in companies. Under his leadership, the group made acquisitions through insolvency legislation and investments in e-commerce, expanded the airline business by winning bids for Air India, and outright bought out AirAsia India. He mentioned that the future strategy is to focus on healthcare, electronics and digital.

Tata-owned Air India got the nod to acquire AirAsia India almost two months after the proposal was made.

The Competition Commission of India (CCI) approved the acquisition of entire shareholding in AirAsia India by Tata-owned Air India.

President:

The Chairman of Tata Sons is usually the Chairman of the Tata Group. As of 2020, the Tata group has had seven presidents. **(PUT THIS INFORMATION IN BOX)**

Jamsetji Tata	(1868-1904)
Sir Dorabji Tata	(1904-1932)
Naoroji Saklatwala	(1932–1938)
JRD Tata	(1938–1991)

Ratan Tata	(1991-2012)
Cyrus Mistry	(2012-2016)
Ratan Tata	(2016-2017)
Natarajan Chandrasekaran	(Present)

Companies acquired by Tata Group:

February 2000	-	Tetley Tea Company, $407 million
March 2004	-	Daewoo Commercial Vehicle Company, $102 million
August 2004	-	NatSteel's steel business, $292 million
November 2004	-	Tyco Global Network, $130 million
July 2005	-	Teleglobe International Holdings, $239 million
October 2005	-	Good Earth Corporation
December 2005	-	Millennium Steel, Thailand, $165 million
December 2005	-	Brunner Mond Chemicals, $10 million
June 2006	-	Eight o'clock coffee, $220 million
November 2006	-	The Ritz Carlton Boston, $170 million
January 2007	-	Chorus Group, $12 billion
March 2007	-	PT Kultim Prima Coal (KPC) (Bumi Resources), $1.1 billion
April 2007	-	Campton Place Hotel, San Francisco, $60 million
January 2008	-	Imacid Chemical Company, Morocco [24]
February 2008	-	General Chemical Industrial Products, $1 billion
March 2008	-	Jaguar Cars and Land Rover, $2.3 billion
March 2008	-	Cerviplaym SA, Spain
April 2008	-	Comoplesa Labrero SA, Spain
May 2008	-	Piaggio Aero Industries Spa, Italy - Sold in 2015

June 2008	-	China Enterprise Communications, China
October 2008	-	Miljo Grenland / Innovasjön, Norway
April 2010	-	Hewitt Robbins International, United Kingdom
July 2013	-	Alti SA, France
December 2014	-	Energy Products Limited, India
June 2016	-	Welspun Renewables Energy, India
May 2018	-	Bhushan Steel Limited, India
February 2021	-	BigBasket (68%) by Tata Digital
June 2021	-	1mg (55%) by Tata Digital
October 2021	-	50% stake in Air India, Air India Express and Air India SATS for ₹18,000 crore (US$2.3 billion).

Companies under Tata Group

Aviation and Defense: Tata Advanced Systems

Information Technology:

Tata Consultancy Services (TCS)

TCS China

TRDDC

CMC Limited

Computational Research Laboratories

Steel:

Tata Steel

Tata Steel Netherlands

Tata Steel UK

Formerly Tata Steel Europe

Tata Steel Long Products

Tata Steel Thailand

Tata Tinplate

Tayo rolls

Jamshedpur FC

Tata Metallics

Power Company:

Tata Power

Tata Power Solar

Nelco Limited

Motor Vehicles :

Tata Motors

Tata Technologies Limited

Jaguar Land Rover

Tata Daewoo

Tata Hispano

Tata Hitachi Construction Machinery

Tata Motors Cars

Consumer & Retail

Tata Chemicals

Tata Chemicals Europe

Tata Salt

Tata Consumer Products :

Good earth tea

Tata Coffee

Tetley

Eight o'clock

Tata Starbucks

Voltas

Titan Company Limited :

    carat lane

    favre-leuba

    fast track

    tanishq

    taneira

Tourism & Travel

    Indian Hotel Company

    Taj Hotel

    Vivanta

    Ginger

    Taj Air

    AirAsia India

    Air India Limited

    Air India

    Air India Express

    Air India SATS Airport Services

Telecom and Media

    Tata Communications VSNL International Canada

    Tata Teleservices

    Tata Play

Trading and Investing:

    Tata International

    Tata Industries Limited

    Tata Health

    Tata Cliq

    Pantone Finvest

Digital

Tata Digital

BigBasket (68%)

Tata 1mg (55%)

Tata New

Infinity Retail

Legal

PLF PVT LTD PLC OF INDIA DIVISION TATA GROUP

Legal Processing Division

Philanthropist:

The Tata Group has helped establish and financed several research, educational and cultural institutions in India, and has received the Carnegie Medal of Philanthropy. Some of the institutions set up by the Tata Group are:

Tata Institute of Fundamental Research

The Energy and Resources Institute (formerly known as Tata Energy and Research Institute), a non-governmental research institute.

JRD Tata Ecotechnology Center

National Center for the Performing Arts

Tata Center for Technology and Design at Massachusetts Institute of Technology

Tata Center for Technology and Design at IIT Bombay

Tata Cricket Academy

Tata Football Academy

Tata Institute of Social Sciences

Tata Management Training Center

Tata Medical Center was inaugurated by Ratan Tata on 16th May 2011.

Tata Memorial Hospital

Tata Cancer Hospital

The Tata Trusts, a group of philanthropic organizations run by the head of the business conglomerate Tata Sons.

In 2008, the Tata Group donated US$50 million to Cornell University "for agricultural and nutrition programs in India and the education of Indian students at Cornell."

In 2010, the Tata Group donated INR 2.20 billion (US$50 million) to Harvard Business School to build an academic and residential building for executive education programs on the institute's campus in Boston, Massachusetts. The building, now known as **Tata Hall,** is the largest endowment received by Harvard Business School from an international donor.

In 2017, Tata Trusts made a US$70 million gift to the University of California, San Diego, along with the establishment of the Tata Institute for Genetics and Society (TIGS) to address some of the world's most pressing issues from public health to agriculture. In recognition of the donation, the building containing the TIGS is named Tata Hall. It is also the largest international donation to the University of California, San Diego.

In 2017, Tata Consultancy Services (TCS) made an unprecedented US$35 million grant to Carnegie Mellon University, the largest industry donation to the university to date, to help promote the next generation of technologies that support cognitive development.

In 2017, Tata Football Academy won the bid to form Jamshedpur FC, a football club based in Jamshedpur, Jharkhand, in the fourth edition of the Indian Super League.

In 2020, the Tata group has donated INR 15 billion to the PM Cares Fund to fight the COVID-19 pandemic in India.

The Tata Group has also attracted some controversies during its 150 years of operation, notably:

Munnar, Kerala:

The Kerala government filed an affidavit in the High Court alleging that Tata Tea "grabbed" 3,000 acres of forest land in Munnar. The Tatas provided that they had 58,741.82 acres of land, which they are allowed to maintain under the **Kannan Devan Hill (Revival of Land) Act, 1971,** and there was a shortfall of 278.23 hectares. He. Kerala Chief Minister vs. Achuthanandan, vowing to evict everyone from government land in

Munnar, formed a special squad for the Munnar Land Acquisition Mission and started taking back properties. However, the mission was canceled due to opposition from both influential landholders and Achuthanandan's own party.

Kalinganagar, Orissa:

On 2nd January 2006, the villagers of Kalinganagar, tribal Orissa, protested the construction of a new steel plant for Tata Steel on land historically owned by them. Some villagers were evicted without adequate relocation. Police retribution was brutal: 37 protesters were injured and 13 killed, including 3 women and a 13-year-old boy. A policeman was killed by a mob after the police fired tear gas and rubber bullets at the protesters. The family members of the deceased villagers later claimed that the bodies were mutilated during the post-mortem.

Supplies to the Burmese Military Regime:

In December 2006, the Chief of General Staff of Myanmar, General Thura Shwe Mann, visited the Tata Motors plant in Pune. In 2009, Tata Motors announced that it would manufacture trucks in Myanmar. Tata Motors reported that these contracts to supply hardware and automobiles to the Burmese military were later criticized by human rights activists.

Singur Land Acquisition:

The Singur controversy in West Bengal was a series of protests by local people and political parties over forced acquisitions, evictions and inadequate compensation to displaced farmers for the Tata Nano plant, during which Mamata Banerjee's party was widely criticized. Despite the support of the Communist Party of India (Marxist) state government, Tata eventually pulled the project out of West Bengal, citing security concerns. Narendra Modi, the then Chief Minister of Gujarat, provided the land for the Nano project.

On August 31st , 2016, in a landmark judgment, the Hon'ble Supreme Court of India quashed the 2006 land acquisition by the Government of West Bengal that had facilitated the Nano plant of Tata Motors, stating that the Government of West Bengal had not taken possession. Lands legally, and were now required to be returned and returned to local farmers within 12 weeks without any compensation.

Dhamra Port, Firoz Krishna:

The port of Dhamara has received significant coverage in India and in Tata's emerging global markets, sparkling controversy. Dhamra port, a similar joint venture between Tata Steel and Larsen & Toubro, has been criticized by Indian and international organizations including Greenpeace for its proximity to Gahirmatha Sanctuary and Bhitarkanika National Park; Gahirmatha Beach is home to one of the world's largest mass nesting sites for Olive Ridley turtles, and India's second largest mangrove forest, Bhitarkanika, is a designated Ramsar site, and critics claimed that the port is part of Gahirmatha beaches. As well as this could disrupt large-scale nesting in the ecology of the Bhitarkanika mangrove forest. Tata Steel employed mitigation measures set by the project's official advisor, the International Union for Conservation of Nature (IUCN) and the company " pledged to adopt all of its recommendations without exception." when conservation organizations insisted that an impact analysis had not been carried out for a complete environmental project, which had changed in size and specifications since it was first proposed.

Proposed Soda Extraction Plant in Tanzania:

In 2007, the Tata Group entered into an alliance with a Tanzanian company to build a soda ash extraction plant in Tanzania. Environmental activists oppose the plant because it would be near Lake Natron, and it has great potential to affect the lake's ecosystem and its neighboring inhabitants, endangering the endangered lesser flamingo birds. Lake Natron is where less than two-thirds of flamingos breed. The production of soda ash involves extracting salt water from the lake and then throwing the water back into the lake. This process can disrupt the chemical makeup of the lake. 22 African countries signed a petition to stop its construction.

In April 2016, a US federal grand jury awarded Epic Systems a US$940 million judgment against Tata Consultancy Services and Tata America International Corp. Filed on 31 October 2014; The lawsuit alleges that " 6,477 unauthorized downloads may have been used to enhance Tata's competing product, Made Mantra." In 2017, US District Court Judge William Conley reduced the award to $420 million; The company says the decision is also being appealed, as "it is not supported by evidence presented during the trial and a stronger appeal can be made to a superior court to outright overturn the jury's decision."

2018 NCLT Verdict:

In July 2018, the National Company Law Tribunal (NCLT), which "addresses issues relating to Indian companies," issued a verdict in favor of the company on allegations of mismanagement leveled in 2016 by ousted chairman Cyrus Mistry.

Ratan Tata's Love: Los Angeles

A few years ago, at an event of the Baroda Management Association (BMA), Ratan Tata had told many things related to his personal life, including his love story. He had told that he fell in love four times in his life, but four times the situation became such that due to one reason or the other, he could not get married. At the same time, he had also said that it was good that he could not get married, if it had happened, the situation would have become more difficult.

This was the biggest secret of Ratan Tata's life. Why didn't he get married yet? There has been a lot of speculation behind this. But he always kept this thing in his heart. Eventually he revealed it, in an interview. In this, he told that after earning an architecture degree from Cornell University he started a job in the city of Los Angeles.

For this job, he spent 2 years there. Then he fell in love with a girl who lived there. He still considers those two years of his life as the best time of his life. They both loved each other very much. Both of them had made up their mind to get married. But then something happened which ended their relationship, forever.

At the same time, the news of his grandmother's ill health reached Ratan Tata. Due to close attachment to his grandmother and not meeting her for 7 years he came back to India. He also asked that woman to accompany him to India. He said that he would go to India and get married. That girl was ready. But his parents did not allow him to go.

This was in the year 1962 when the war between India and China was going on. Due to this war, the parents of that girl refused to let them go. So, the woman promised to come to India as soon as the war was over. With this belief, Ratan Tata returned back to his grandmother. He came to India and waited for the woman. He was sure that she would definitely come to him. His wait got longer. At last, they got the news. The woman's parents got her married to someone else.

Hearing this news, he was deeply shocked. His heart was completely broken. Because he had truly loved that woman. He had also promised that he would marry her.For Ratan Tata, it became the reason for not getting married for the rest of his life. This proves that Ratan Tata was so firm in his promises and principles. This is the biggest reason for their success.

Ratan Tata is very fond of reading books, especially success stories. In an interview, he had told that after retirement he would focus more on reading books. Apart from this, he is also very fond of keeping dogs. He has shared pictures of his pet dogs many times on social media.

Ratan Tata also keeps sharing the ghosts of his personal life on his Facebook page 'Humans of Bombay.' He has also mentioned his love story on this page.

Ratan Tata's Achievements, Honors and Awards

Ratanji Bhai Tata is a role model in himself. He has been honored with various honors by the Government of India and various foreign governments. Here we will discuss some of the awards and honors received by him. And you will find how one person can get so many honors and rewards in his life. This cannot be an ordinary man. Yes it is true that Ratanji Bhai is above any ordinary man. He provides a new direction to our society and also gives an inspiration to the youth. Let us go ahead by mentioning these honors.

Ratan Tata received the **Padma Bhushan** in 2000 and the **Padma Vibhushan** in 2008, the third and second highest civilian honors given by the Government of India. In 2021 he received Assam's highest civilian award **'Assam Baibhav'** for his exceptional contribution in advancing cancer care in Assam.

Other awards include:

2001 Honorary Doctor of Business Administration awarded by Ohio State University:

It is an honorary doctorate of Business Administration or a professional doctorate or a research doctorate, awarded on the basis of advanced study, examinations, project work and research in business administration.

2004 Medal of the Oriental Republic of Uruguay awarded by the Government of Uruguay

It is given by the President of Uruguay at the initiative of the Ministry of Foreign Affairs.

The Medal of the Oriental Republic of Uruguay is a distinguished award of Uruguay created by Law No. 16300.

2004 Honorary Doctor of Technology by Asian Institute of Technology

Doctor of Technology is a degree usually awarded to candidates after a course of study in technology and a dissertation or completion of a long-term project in a technically related field. Like other doctorates, it is usually an academic degree at the highest level equivalent to a PhD.

While degree details vary, a doctor of technology program typically enables graduates to acquire an advanced level of knowledge in specialist areas and aims to produce graduates capable of advancing knowledge within their industry. The degree focuses on developing practical solutions in the workplace, critical analysis, synthesis and innovation.

Tata has been given this award by the Asian Institute of Technology The Asian Institute of Technology (AIT), established in 1959, is an international organization for higher education located 40 km north of Bangkok, Thailand. It specializes in engineering, advanced technologies, sustainable development, and management and planning. It aims to "promote technological change and sustainable development" in the Asia-Pacific region through higher education, research and outreach.

2005 International Distinguished Achievement Award by Brith International

Brith International is a Jewish service organization. Bnei Brith says it is committed to the security and continuity of the Jewish people and the State of Israel and combats anti-Semitism and other forms of bigotry.

2005 Honorary Doctor of Science by the University of Warwick

Doctor of Science is commonly abbreviated to Sc. D, D.Sc. Deed, also called DS or DS, is an academic research degree awarded in many countries around the world. In some countries "Doctor of Science" is a degree used for standard doctorates in science; Elsewhere S.D. is a "higher doctorate" awarded in recognition of a substantial and continuing contribution beyond the scientific knowledge required for a Doctor of Philosophy (PhD). Tata was awarded this degree by the University of Warwick.

The University of Warwick is a public research university on the outskirts of Coventry, between the West Midlands and Warwickshire, England. The university was established in 1965 as part of a government initiative to expand higher education.

2006 Honorary Doctor of Science by Indian Institute of Technology Madras

2006 Responsible Capitalism Award for Inspiration and Recognition of Science and Technology

For the inspiration and recognition of Science and Technology (First) is an international youth organization that organizes the first Robotics Competition, the first Lego League Challenge, the first Lego League Explore, the first Lego League Discover, and the first Tech Challenge competitions. Founded in 1989 by Dean Kamen and Woody Flowers, its express goal is to develop ways to inspire students in the engineering and technology fields. Its philosophy is expressed by the organization: **Cooperation and Racial Professionalism**. FIRST also operates FIRST Place, a research facility at FIRST Headquarters in Manchester, New Hampshire, where it organizes educational programs and day camps for students and teachers.

Honorary Fellowship in 2007 by the London School of Economics and Political Science

Honorary degrees in academia (professor, reader, lecturer) may be awarded to individuals in recognition of contributions by non-employees or an employee beyond regular duties. The practice exists primarily in the UK and Germany, as well as in many universities and colleges in the United States, Australia, Hong Kong, Taiwan, China, New Zealand, Japan, Denmark and Canada.

Some other examples of such titles are Honorary Professor, Honorary Fellow, Honorary Senior Research Fellow, Honorary Reader, Honorary Lecturer (usually applied to non-teaching staff, who occasionally lecture), Visiting Fellow (usually Applies to students taking on) further study and research programmes), Industrial Fellow.

The institution awarding this fellowship is the London School of Economics and Political Science (LSE or LSE), a public research university located in London, England, and a constituent college of the Federal University of London.

2007 Carnegie Medal of Philanthropy is awarded for International Peace

The Carnegie Medal of Philanthropy is a personal award for philanthropy, given every other year by the Carnegie family institutions to a number of individuals. In recent years the medal has been presented in New York.

2008 Honorary Doctorate of Law awarded by the University of Cambridge

Doctor of Law is a degree in Law. The use of the term varies from country to country and includes such names as Doctor of Juridical Science (JSD or SJD), Juris Doctor (JD), Doctor of Philosophy (Ph.D.), and Legum Doctor (LL.D.). degrees are included. ,

2008 Honorary Doctorate of Science awarded by Indian Institute of Technology Bombay

The Indian Institute of Technology Bombay (IIT Bombay or IITB) is an internationally acclaimed autonomous public research university and technical institute in Powai, Mumbai, Maharashtra, India.

2008 Honorary Doctor of Science degree conferred by Indian Institute of Technology Kharagpur

Indian Institute of Technology Kharagpur (IIT Kharagpur) is a public research university established by the Government of India in Kharagpur, West Bengal, India. Established in 1951, the institute is the first IIT to be established and is recognized as an Institute of National Importance. In 2019, it was given the status of Institute of Eminence by the Government of India.

2008 Honorary Citizen Award by the Government of Singapore

The Honorary Civilian Award is the highest national honor given by the Government of Singapore to foreigners since 2003, to recognize and acknowledge the contributions of foreigners who have made large and significant contributions to Singapore and its people.

2008 Honorary Fellowship is awarded by the Institute of Engineering and Technology

Institution of Engineering and Technology (IET) is a multidisciplinary professional engineering institute. The IET was formed in 2006 from two separate institutions: the Institution of Electrical Engineers (IEE), 1871 and the Institution of Incorporated Engineers (IIE) in 1884. It currently has a worldwide membership of 153 countries. IET's main offices are at Savoy Place in London, England, and Michael Faraday House in Stevenage, England.

The Inspired Leadership Award in 2008 is an award given by Performance Theatre.

2009 Honorary Knight Commander of the Order of the British Empire (KBE) by Queen Elizabeth The Most Outstanding Order of the British Empire is a British order of chivalry, which rewards contributions to the arts and sciences, work with charitable and charitable organizations, and does public service outside the civil service. It was established on 4 June 1917 by King George V

And it includes five classes in both the civilian and military divisions.

The Life Time Contribution Award in Engineering for 2009 in 2008 is given by Indian National Academy of Engineering

Established in 1987, the Indian National Academy of Engineering (INAE) comprises engineers, engineer-scientists and technologists from India covering the entire spectrum of engineering disciplines. The Academy is registered under the **Societies Registration Act 1860** and is an autonomous institution partially supported through grant-in-aid by the Department of Science and Technology, Government of India. As the only engineering academy in the country, INAE represents India in the International Council of Academy of Engineering and Technical Sciences (CAETS). INAE acts as an apex body and promotes the practice of engineering and technology and related sciences for their application to solve problems of national importance. The Academy also provides a platform for future planning for the country's development, which requires engineering and technical inputs and brings together experts from such fields as may be necessary for a comprehensive solution to the country's needs.

2009 Grand Officer of the Order of Merit of the Italian Republic is conferred by the Government of Italy

The Order of Merit of the Italian Republic (Italian: Ordin al merito della Repubblica Italiana) is the Senior Italian Merit of Merit. It was founded in 1951 by Luigi Einaudi, the second President of the Italian Republic.

The Republic's highest-ranking honour, it is awarded for "merit earned by the nation" in the fields of literature, art, economy, public service, and social, philanthropic and humanitarian activities, and for long and distinguished service in civilian life. The letters after the nominal for the order are OMRI.

Honorary Doctor of Laws conferred by the University of Cambridge in 2010

2010 Hadrian Prize by the World Memorial Fund

The World Monuments Fund (WMF) is a private, international, non-profit organization dedicated to the conservation of historic architectural and cultural heritage sites around the world through field work, advocacy, grants, education and training.

Founded in 1965, WMF is headquartered in New York, and has offices and affiliates around the world, including Cambodia, France, Peru, Portugal, Spain, and the United Kingdom. In addition to practical management, collaborators identify, develop and manage projects, negotiate local partnerships, and attract local support to supplement funds provided by donors.

2010 for Oslo Business Peace Foundation for Peace Prize

Business for Peace (BFP) is a non-profit foundation based in Oslo, Norway. In recognition of their personal and business-worthy contributions to building trust, stability and peace, each year, the Foundation nominates seven honorable people who receive the Oslo Business for Peace Award. Honorees are selected by an independent committee, made up of winners of either the Nobel Peace Prize or the Nobel Memorial Prize in Economic Sciences.

The Foundation works around the world to understand how ethical and responsible business can contribute to building trust, stability and peace. Every year, the Foundation organizes the Oslo Business for Peace Summit, which culminates with the presentation of the award to that year's honorees.

2010 Legend in Leadership Award by Yale University

Yale University is a private Ivy League research university in New Haven, Connecticut. Founded in 1701 as a collegiate school, it is the third oldest institution of higher education in the United States and the most prestigious in the world.

2010 Honorary Doctorate of Law awarded by Pepperdine University

Pepperdine University is a private research university affiliated with the Church of Christ.

In 2010 the Peace Prize was given by the Peace Foundation.

Business Leader of the Year Award Asian Award in 2010.

The Asian Awards was founded by businessman Paul Sagoo through his Lemon Group.

The Asian Awards is an annual award ceremony for the global Asian community that takes place in the United Kingdom, in 14 categories including business, philanthropy, entertainment, culture and sport. Nominees are selected by an independent judging panel, initially co-chaired by Baroness Verma and Nat Wei, Baron Wei, then from 2014 onwards by Karan Billimoria, Baron Billimoria.

In 2010 and 2011, the awards were open only to those born in or directly into a family from India, Sri Lanka, Pakistan or Bangladesh. From 2013, they were expanded to include all people of South, East and South-east Asian descent.

The tenth edition of the awards will take place in 2023 due to the COVID-19 pandemic.

Honorary Fellow of the Royal Academy of Engineering in 2012.

The Royal Academy of Engineering (RAEng) is the national academy of engineering of the United Kingdom.

In 2012 Honorary Doctor of Business Awarded by the University of New South Wales.

The University of New South Wales (UNSW), also known as UNSW Sydney, is a public research university located in Sydney, New South Wales, Australia. It is one of the founding members of the Group of Eight, a coalition of Australian research-intensive universities.

2012 Grand Cardon of the Order of the Rising Sun by the Government of Japan

The Order of the Rising Sun is a Japanese order, established by Emperor Meiji in 1875. The order was the first national embellishment granted by the Japanese government, created by order of the Council of State on 10th April 1875. This badge has the rays of the sun emanating from the rising sun. The Rising Sun design symbolizes the powerful energy of the rising sun parallel to Japan's concept of "Rising Sun" ("Land of the Rising Sun").

Given by the National Academy of Engineering for Foreign Collaboration in 2013.

Awarded the title of **Transformational Leader of the Decade** in 2013 at the Indian Affairs India Leadership Conclave 2013.

2013 Ernst & Young Entrepreneur of the Year - Lifetime Achievement by Ernst & Young.

Ernst & Young Global Limited, trade name EY, is a multinational professional services partnership headquartered in London, England. EY is one of the largest professional service networks in the world. Along with Deloitte, KPMG and PricewaterhouseCoopers, it is considered one of the Big Four accounting firms. It primarily provides assurance (including financial audit), tax, consulting and advisory services to its clients. Like many large accounting firms in recent years, EY has expanded into markets adjacent to accounting, including strategy, operations, human resources, technology and financial services consulting.

Given by the University of Melon to confer an Honorary Doctorate of Business Practice in 2013.

Carnegie Mellon University (CMU) is a private research university located in Pittsburgh, Pennsylvania.

Honorary Doctor of Business degree conferred by Singapore Management University in 2014.

In 2014, Sayaji Ratna Award was given by Baroda Management Association.

The Baroda Management Association (BMA) has instituted a national level Sayaji Ratna Award in 2013 to mark the 151st birth anniversary of Maharaja Sayajirao Gaekwad III, the then ruler of Baroda. BMA is an organization established in 1957 in Vadodara and is an organization member of All India Management Association. The award is given annually to the living stalwarts of India. It recognizes personality of eminent character and outstanding contribution in the fields of business, sports, arts, humanity, education, governance and medicine. The jury selects a man whose life exhibited such stellar qualities that Maharaja Sayajirao

III imbibed and displayed during his illustrious reign. Important among those qualities are vision, integrity, compassion, philanthropy, institution building ability, mentorship and leadership of experts that touches, inspires and uplifts all sections of society.

Honorary Knight Grand Cross of the Order of the British Empire (GBE) by Queen Elizabeth in 2014.

In 2014 Honorary Doctorate of Law conferred by the University of York, Canada.

In 2015 Honorary Doctorate of Automotive Engineering awarded by Clemson University.

2015 Sayaji Ratna Award by Baroda Management Association, Honoris Causa, HEC Paris

Baroda Management Association (BMA) is an autonomous, professional, non-political and non-profit body based in Vadodara, Gujarat, India. It is affiliated to All India Management Association, Delhi and is registered under Bombay Public Trust Act, 1950. It was established on 29th May 1957 by prominent managers and industrialists. In 2012-13, it crossed Rs 1 crore as revenue. The BMA instituted a national level Sayaji Ratna award in 2013 to mark the 151st birth anniversary of Maharaja Sayajirao Gaekwad III. The recipients are NR Narayana Murthy, Ratan Tata and Amitabh Bachchan.

In 2016 the Commander of the Legion of Honour, presented by the Government of France.

Founded in 1802 by Napoleon Bonaparte.

In 2018 an honorary doctorate was given by Swansea University.

Honorary Doctorate of Literature in 2022 given by HSNC University.

Ratan Tata: A Unique Personality

Ratan Tata reduced the number of companies in the Tata Group to less than 300 to invest in newly emerging businesses that showed potential for growth. Ratan Tata is a true visionary in every way. The Tata Group acquired several foreign brands to expand its reach. For example, Tata Tea acquired UK-based brand Tetley in 2000 for $407 million. Tetley is sold as Tata Tea which is a product of Tata Consumer Products Limited. It is now sold in over 40 countries worldwide.

He started various companies under his supervision and earned huge revenue. Tata Son's salt-to-software ventures turned into a $100 billion conglomerate under Ratan Tata.

Under Ratan Tata's initiative, Tata Motors acquired Daewoo Commercial Vehicles in 2004 for $102 million. This was the largest acquisition of a Korean company by an Indian company. In 2007, Ratan Tata acquired Corus, an Anglo-Dutch steel maker, for $12.2 billion. The deal made Tata-Corus the fifth largest steel maker in the world.

Ratan Tata's sharp business acumen was proved again a year later, when Tata Motors acquired two British car brands, Jaguar and Land Rover. It was a takeover with Ford that cost Tata $2.3 billion. It was Ratan Tata who drove the entire acquisition drive, and in 2017, JLR's revenue topped $34 billion.

In 2008, Ratan Tata, who launched the world's cheapest car, the Tata Nano, added another feather to the cap. The Nano was launched at an Auto Expo and became the subject of case studies in all the top-B schools across the world.

Once, during heavy rains in Mumbai, Ratan Tata saw a family of four riding a bike. Two children were riding bikes with their parents in heavy rain. The children were sandwiched between father and mother. This sparked the idea of coming up with an affordable car for the lower middle class consumers who are taking the brunt of the weather. To bring relief in the lives of such people, Ratan Tata invented the Tata Nano.

Ratan Tata has been an outstanding leader with sharp decisiveness, fairness, enthusiasm, integrity, endurance and business acumen. He served the Tata Group for 50 years. At the age of 75, he retired as the chairman of the Tata Group in 2012, after hiring a suitable person 'to fill the gap. Ratan Tata's successor was Cyrus Mistry, son of Pallonji Mistry of the Shapoorji Pallonji Group. He was the largest individual shareholder of the group.

But, Cyrus Mistry was suddenly removed from the post in 2016. His sudden removal was heavily scrutinized by the media. Ratan Tata was immediately appointed interim chairman. A large selection committee was formed to appoint the new chairman.Mr Tata, Amit Chandra of Bain Capital, TVS Group chief Venu Srinivasan, former diplomat Ronen Sen and Lord Kumar Bhattacharya. On 12th January 2017, Natarajan Chandrasekaran was named as the chairman of Tata Sons.

Nothing has changed after the retirement of Ratan Tata, as he followed strong policies, practices and SOPs under his tenure. Ratan Tata is still actively involved in looking for new start-ups for investment. He has recently bought stake in several start-ups which are showing potential for growth. Ratan Tata is also actively involved in the Tata Trust which is a charitable Tata organization. Tata Trusts aims to overcome child malnutrition, health care, social justice and health care.

Unfortunately, soon after Ratan Tata took over as chairman, he faced considerable resistance from other top Tata executives. Many of them had been working in companies under the Tata Group for decades and had become very powerful. This was also partly due to the fact that JRD Tata had given him too much freedom.

Ratan Tata faced this opposition boldly instead of his opponents by setting an official retirement age. He further asked the individual companies under the Tata Group to report operations to the group office. He also collected some funds from each company to grow and strengthen the Tata brand.

Ratan Tata, though inherited his position from his predecessors, was experienced enough to handle his craft. He gave great priority to innovative thinking and young talents were hired and given responsibilities. His leadership ensured that all operations were conducted to create a synergy in working. All irrelevant businesses were shut down by Ratan Tata to target the foreign market. In 1991, JRD Tata retired as chairman, naming Ratan Tata as his successor.

Tata as India's largest trading brand:

Tata was started in the year 1868. Since then, it has grown by leaps and bounds. Today, if you list the top companies in India, 4 out of 5 companies belong to the Tata Group. Tata gained its global recognition by collaborating with several international brands.

There are 96 brands operating under Tata's umbrella, out of which 36 are publicly listed such as Titan, Tata Steel, etc. The total market capitalization is approximately $130 billion.

Tata's Business Strategies:

The first 21 years of Ratan Tata leading the Tata Group as Chairman set new benchmarks for the company's success. Tata's revenue grew more than 40 times and its profits increased by more than 50 times. Tata's business strategies of acquiring promising global brands helped Tata emerge as a global leader. Tata was no longer confined within Indian borders, but his collaborations with Tetley and Chorus demonstrated his potential to the world.

65% of Tata's revenue came from sales in over 100 countries around the world. It was Ratan Tata's sharp business acumen that led to the creation of the Tata Nano. He wanted to launch a car within the reach of an Indian consumer, which he revealed in an interview to the Harvard Business School Emerging Markets Project.

Tata also ventured into **Snapdeal** (India's leading e-commerce website) in 2016, **Teabox** (online premium tea seller), and **Cashkaro.com** (a discount coupon and cash-back website). Ratan Tata evaluates business investment opportunities and invests in companies at early and later stages.

He invested 0.95 crores in **Ola Cabs**, an upcoming promising venture. In April 2015, Tata partnered with Chinese smartphone **Xiaomi.** In October 2015, Tata partnered with American Express, and invested in the bitcoin venture **Abra**. In 2016, Ratan Tata invested in **Nestaway**, an online real estate portal for singles to search for fully furnished flats. Nestaway later acquired **Zenify** to enter the family rental market segment and online pet care portal **Dogspot.**

In addition to these investments, led by Ratan Tata, Tata Motors invented its first batch of Tata electric vehicles. These vehicles are manufactured in Gujarat. The Indian government has an ambitious target of having only electric cars on Indian roads by 2030.

Ratan Tata: One of the world's leading philanthropists

Ratan Tata is a prominent philanthropist of India. He is actively engaged in social welfare in other countries as well. Tata invests a lot of money in education, rural development and healthcare.

Tata financed the development of capacitive deionization at the University of New South Wales' engineering faculty to provide water for challenging areas.

The Tata Trusts gave a scholarship fund of $28 million to Cornell University to provide financial assistance to undergraduate Indian students. These scholarships allow up to 20 students to pursue undergraduate courses at Cornell University regardless of their financial health. The scholarship will be awarded annually and recipients will receive the scholarship for the entire duration of their undergraduate studies at Cornell.

In 2010, the Tata Group contributed a whopping $50 million to build an executive center at Harvard Business School (HBS). The Executive Hall at HBS has been named 'Tata Hall' to honor Ratan Tata. The hall cost $100 million to build is used for mid-career executive educational programs. The hall is seven storeys tall and has an area of approximately 155,000 gross square feet. This hall has 180 bedrooms along with academic and multi-purpose spaces.

Tata donated $35 million to Carnegie Mellon University for research into cognitive systems and autonomous vehicles. Using this donation a hall was built in an area of 48,000 sq ft and it was named TCS Hall.

In 2014, the Tata Group made the largest ever donation in Indian history of $950 million to the Indian Institute of Technology, Bombay. Using this money, a formal Tata Center for Technology and Design (TCTD) has been created to develop design and engineering principles for the upliftment of communities with limited resources.

The Tata Group also contributed to the development of the MIT Tata Center of Technology and Design at the Massachusetts Institute of Technology (MIT). The center was developed to address the challenges of resource-constrained communities with an initial focus on India.

Ratan Tata launched an in-home water-purification device called **Tata Swach** for just Rs.1000.

When the 26/11 attacks devastated the world, Tata came forward and supported its employees during the terrorist attack, by ensuring that the employees received their salaries on time. Due to the chaos, the hotels were dysfunctional but Tata ensured that its employees did not suffer its financial loss.

Tata is extremely conscious of its employee welfare. He designed modern pension system and introduced maternity leave, medical facilities and other benefits for the welfare of his employees all over the country. Ratan Tata also gave money to employees of railways, market vendors, police stations, including pedestrians.

Ratan Tata, in one of his recent efforts, announced a $70 million donation towards the creation of the **Tata Institute of Genetics and Society** in Bengaluru. This center will work to modify the DNA of mosquitoes to eliminate malaria from India. Ratan Tata will be the trustee of this institute.

When COVID-19 suddenly emerged, Tata Trusts announced a donation of Rs 500 crore to buy PPE kits and other essentials to fight the infection.

Ratan Tata's Vision

In the words of Ratan Tata, "What I want to do is leave behind a permanent entity of a group of companies that work exemplary in terms of ethics, values and what our forefathers have left behind. "

Ratan Tata has strictly protected the brand image of Tata. Under his leadership, Tata has always been making headlines for all the right reasons. Tata is the largest commercial brand which has contributed immensely to the growth and development of India. In one of his recent unique endeavors, Ratan Tata penned down some insights into how businesses should be doing post COVID-19. He did this to help propel millions of businesses out of the sudden pandemic storm. Ratan Tata is indeed an inspiration to the world and youths look up to him.

Board Membership and Affiliation:

You will be surprised to know that about 66 percent of Tata Sons is held by charitable trusts, which are controlled by the members of the Tata family. Two of the largest trusts are the **Sir Ratan Tata Trust** and the **Sir Dorabji Tata Trust.**

Ratan Tata has worked in various capacities in India and abroad. He is an active member of the Prime Minister's Council on Trade and Industry and the National Manufacturing Competitiveness Council.

Ratan Tata is on the jury panel of the world's leading architectural prize, the **Pritzker Architecture Prize.**

Ratan Tata is a Director on the Board of Governors of Alcoa Inc., Mondelez International and East-West Center. Since 2006, Ratan Tata is also a member of the Harvard Business School India Advisory Board (IAB), and previously a member of the Harvard Business School Asia-Pacific Advisory Board (APAB) 2001–2006.

In 2013, he was appointed to the board of trustees of the Carnegie Endowment for International Peace. Ratan Tata also played an advisory role at Kalaari Capital, a venture capital firm founded by Vani Kola. Ratan Tata is also a member of the Board of Trustees of the University of Southern California, Harvard Business School Board of Dean Advisors, X Prize and Cornell University. Ratan Tata is also on the board of the International Advisory Council at Bocconi University.

Ratan Tata's Wealth

Ratan Tata's net worth:

Ratan Tata's net worth is $1 billion which is equal to Rs. 7416 crore in Indian currency. His monthly income is 90+ crores and his annual income is 820+ crores.

Ratan Tata's assets:

Ratan Tata has a house in Mumbai (India) where he lives. He bought this luxury house in the year 2015. The cost of this house is estimated to be around Rs 150 crores. He is the owner of many properties across India.

Ratan Tata owns many cars, some of which are the best luxury cars in the world. He owns Cadillac XLR, Mercedes Benz, Range Rover, Honda Civic, Maserati Quattroporte, Chrysler Sebring, Ferrari, Buick Super 8, Jaguar and Tata.

Is Ratan Tata the richest man in the world? ,

The answer to this question is, 'No, Ratan Tata is not the richest man in the world'. Despite having a staggering business that is bigger than Bill Gates or Mark Zuckerberg or Jeff Bezos, Ratan Tata is not the richest man.

Well, there is an interesting story behind it. Ratan Tata is a man of ideologies, ethics and values. He is not related to his success by getting a spot in the top list of Forbes but genuinely believes in giving back to the society.

Would you believe that Ratan Tata donates 65% of his money to charitable causes? Any revenue generated around the world never affects his personal account, but is given to charitable organizations.

His personal wealth never exceeds the $1 billion mark.

Interesting Facts

Ratan Tata is also a trained pilot. He has a license to fly an F-16. He is the first citizen to hold such a license.

Ratan Tata wanted to marry a girl whom he fell in love with while working in New York. But, destiny played its part, as he had to go back to India to be with his ailing grandmother and the girl refused to be with him.

Tata is very fond of animals. Tradition has it that the headquarters of Tata Sons has a kennel for stray dogs, which allows them to come during the rainy season.

Ratan Tata initially joined Tata when he was given the task of managing the blast furnace and removing the limestone. His first job was managing operations on the shop floor of Tata Steel in 1961.

It was because of Tata's practical business acumen, he led mergers and acquisitions with several business conglomerates that skyrocketed Tata's revenues.

Ratan Tata earned his morals from his grandmother, who raised him after his parents separated. He learned from her to stand with dignity in every adversity. He gives the biggest moral lesson of his life to his grandmother.

In 2009, he conceived the Tata Nano car, India's cheapest car, priced at Rs 1 lakh and launched it in the market. Tata Nano enhanced Tata's capability globally.

Ratan Tata is indeed a man of ethics and principles. The biggest lesson he has taught us is that no matter what happens, never compromise on your principles and ethics.

Ten Inspirations from Ratan Tata's Life

Known for his vision and business mind, Ratan Tata has been inspiring thousands of leaders and entrepreneurs across the country. Despite retiring, he is still working as an investor. He has seen a lot of ups and downs in life - unsuccessful ventures and losses in his professional life. But, like a true fighter, he has always managed to overcome all odds. His struggle and charismatic leadership helped the Tata Group to become one of the largest conglomerates in India.

Let us take a dose of inspiration from the life of Ratan Tata.

1. Have a look

Mr. Ratan Tata always had a vision for his organization and himself. When he joined the group, he was barely doing any business outside India. Despite protests, he said the company has to go global. Ratan Tata once said, "If you want to walk fast, walk alone." But if you want to walk far, then walk together." Mr. Tata's ambitious vision of building a car for the common man that costs only 1 lakh - the "Nano" - is his vision of envisioning the needs and demands of society.

2. Don't be afraid to take risks

As a leader, one needs foresight and risk taking ability to take the company to new heights. Ratan Tata had the courage to take risks. "I don't believe in taking right decisions," he says. I make decisions and then correct them."

3. Be creative. Be amazing

These words of Ratan Tata reflect one of the core truths of life - "We all do not have equal talent. Yet, we all have equal opportunity to develop our talent." You all have your own unique creative sense and instead of wondering what you don't have, take advantage of every opportunity to showcase your talents and see how your creativity will make you emerge as a winner.

4. Failures are the steps to success

You fail only when you stop pushing yourself harder. Ratan Tata has said that "the ups and downs in life are very important to keep us going, because even a straight line in the ECG means we are not alive". He always loves to lead an exciting life which provides you with versatile learning experiences. No matter how many times you fall, what matters is how firmly you stand on your feet.

5. Ignore all criticism

Being open to criticism, Mr. Tata once said, "Take the stones people throw at you and use them to build a monument." Whenever you try to do something you like, then there will be people who will try to bring you down and criticize you for destroying your soul. All you have to do is ignore all the criticism and focus on your work.

6. Never look back and regret your past mistakes

Many people like to delve into the past in their spare time and think about all the unfortunate things that could have happened if they had acted differently. But this unproductive work only weakens the souls. Ratan Tata says, "There are so many things that if I want to live again, I'll probably do it another way. But I don't want to look back and think about what I couldn't do.

7. Have a positive attitude and mindset

Mr. Ratan Tata always had a positive attitude and had a smile on his face, no matter what the situation. He says, "No one can destroy iron, but its own can rust! Similarly, no one can destroy a person, but his own mindset can." Having a positive attitude and attitude is essential to keeping your focus on your dreams and desired tasks.

8. Believe in yourself

Mr. Tata always believed in himself and what he was doing. When you are dealing with the messes of life, every minute you make a decision.

Some decisions are right while some decisions are such that circumstances can take an unexpected turn. Don't lose your faith if you are working on something valuable. We need to learn that it takes time for every innovation to succeed.

9. Share your stories to inspire others

Ratan Tata had the ability to motivate his team to do the work effectively and efficiently, which is very important for a leader. He always had a habit of sharing his stories to inspire others to achieve. Being a great leader you need to make sure that you inspire, drive and awaken your drive to others, so that they can bring change, social innovation and progress along with you.

10. Be very flexible in decision-making

Too many entrepreneurs put a lot of effort and time on a plan, even when it is not working. Ratan Tata's life shows that one should be very flexible in decision-making. Mr. Tata believed in investing in various companies so that their investment is always safe and there is no growth in the status of a particular industry. He is still following this principle.

Life Changing Quotes of Ratan Tata

"Ups and downs in life are very important to keep us going because even a straight line in the ECG means we are not alive."

"Life is very boring and dull without excitement, ups and downs. You need to be your grandchildren's storyteller, why not prepare for that now? We get this life only once, we experience every aspect of it. No one has ever grown without falling once, fail as many times as possible, only then can you succeed. So stop complaining and start investigating."

"Take stones for people to throw at you, and use them to build monuments."

"We always complain about some external factor for our failure and misery. But the reality is that none of them affect your dreams until you give them the power to do so. Focus on what you want to do and move on, success will not be far from you."

"No one can destroy iron, but its own can rust! Similarly, no one can destroy a person, but he can have his own mindset!"

"I have always been very confident and very excited about India's future potential. I think it is a great country with great potential."

"All the people you meet in this life will not be good for you. Some will criticize, some will discourage you and some will try to put you down. All you have to do is ignore them and move on. They don't need to explain their journey nor do they need to control their dreams. It's your life, live as you want."

"We do not all have the same talent. Yet, we all have the same opportunity to develop our talents."

"If you want to go fast, walk alone. But if you want to go far, walk along."

"Life is unfair and it's not written anywhere to be fair. But it's not just you or me, but for everyone. My talent is different from yours and your talent from other person, but we have our own - There are equal opportunities to be successful in their fields. Where there is six, there is staying."

"The strong live and the weak die. Some bloodshed has taken place, and from this emerges a leaner industry, which tends to survive."

"Stop taking baby steps and start thinking globally."

"There are so many things, if I want to live again, I'll probably do it another way. But I don't want to look back and think about what I couldn't do."

"The day I am not able to fly will be a sad day for me."

"I may have hurt a few people along the way, but I would like to be seen as someone who has tried my best to do the right thing for any situation and doesn't compromise."

"I don't believe in making right decisions, I make decisions and then correct them."

"Encourage people, question unquestioningly and don't be shy to bring up new ideas, new processes to get things done."

Cyrus Mistry

Before knowing about Cyrus Mistry it is necessary to discuss here about his father who is very closely related to Tata family and worked as part of Tata Group.

Cyrus Mistry's father Pallonji Shapoorji Mistry (1st June 1929 – 28th June 2022) was an Indian-born Irish billionaire construction tycoon. He was the chairman of the Shapoorji Pallonji Group and a major shareholder of the Tata Group, India's largest private conglomerate. He was one of the richest people in the world.

Pallonji Mistry was born on 1st June 1929 in Bombay (now Mumbai) to Shapoorji Mistry. He was a member of the Parsi community in Bombay.

Mistry owns a large construction company, Shapoorji Pallonji. Shapoorji, the group's head and Pallonji's father, built some of Mumbai's landmarks around the Fort area - the Hong Kong and Shanghai Bank, Grindlays Bank, Standard Chartered Bank, State Bank of India and Reserve Bank of India buildings.

Career:

His father first bought shares in Tata Sons in the 1930s, a stake that stood at 18.4% by 2011, making Mistry the largest individual shareholder in Tata Sons, which is primarily controlled by the Tata Philanthropic Associate Trusts, and India. The largest individual shareholder in the U.S.'s largest private conglomerate, the Tata Group, the primary shareholder is the charitable Tata Trusts.

Pallonji Mistry was the chairman of the Shapoorji Pallonji Group, through which he owned Shapoorji Pallonji Construction Limited, Forbes Textiles and Eureka Forbes Limited. He was the former Chairman of Associated Cement Companies.

His son, Cyrus, was the chairman of Tata Sons from November 2011 to October 2016. Within the Tata Group, he is known as the **Phantom of**

Bombay House for his calm but confident manner of commanding power around the Mumbai headquarters.

According to the Bloomberg Billionaires Index, Pallonji Mistry's wealth was estimated to be around US\$30 billion in mid-2021 and US\$29 billion at the time of his death. He was the richest Irish billionaire at the time of his death, and the 143rd richest person in the world.

Personal Life and Death:

In 2003, Pallonji renounced his Indian citizenship to become an Irish citizen "on the basis of marriage to an Irish citizen", Pat "Patsy" Perrin Dubash, who was born in September 1939 at Hatch Street Nursing House in Dublin. He lived in his residence in Mumbai. The family's interest in Ireland is due, in part, to their love for horses; Mistry has a 200-acre (0.81 km) stud farm and 10,000 square feet (930 m) home in Pune, India.

Mistry has two sons and two daughters. His elder son, Shapoor Mistry (b. 1964), runs the Shapoorji Pallonji Group, while his younger son, the late Cyrus Mistry (1968–2022), served for a few years as the chairman of the Tata Group. Mistry's elder daughter is Laila and his younger daughter Aloo is married to Ratan Tata's half-brother, Noel Tata.

He was awarded the **Padma Bhushan** by the Government of India in January 2016 for his contribution in the field of trade and industry.

A short biography of Mistry was written in Manoj Namburu's book, **The Moguls of Real Estate** in 2008.

Mistry passed away at the age of 93 on June 28th , 2022 in Mumbai

He held 18.4% stake in Tata Sons through his company **Cyrus Investment Pvt Ltd.** According to the Limited Bloomberg Billionaires Index, Mistry's net worth at the time of his death was approximately \$29 billion, making him one of the richest men in India. He was a member of the National Integration Council. He died in a road accident on the Ahmedabad-Mumbai highway on 4th September 2022. The forensic investigation team attributed the accident to poor road design near the bridge at the accident site.

Early Life and Education:

Mistry was born on 4th July 1968 in Bombay (now Mumbai), Maharashtra, into a Parsi family, the younger son of Indian billionaire and construction businessman Pallonji Mistry, by his wife Patsy Perrin Dubash. Both his parents are of Parsi faith and have roots in India. However, Mistry's mother was born in Ireland, and her father opted to take up Irish citizenship. Mistry had an elder brother, Shapoor Mistry, who is also an Irish citizen, and is married to Behrouz Sethna, daughter of Parsi lawyer, Rusi Sethna. Mistry also has two sisters, Laila and Aloo. Laila is married to Rustam Jehangir, a London-based portfolio fund manager. Aloo is married to Ratan Tata's half-Indian-Parsi, half-French-Catholic half-brother, Noel Tata.

The Pallonji family has been active in the business for more than a century, and in the 1930s Mistry's grandfather Shapoorji Mistry first acquired a stake in Tata Sons. The stake, which now stands at 18.5%, was held by Mistry's father, and comprises the largest block of shares held by a single party; About 66% stake in Tata Sons is controlled by charitable trusts set up by the family. The Egyptians grew up in prosperous conditions.

Mistry was educated at the prestigious Cathedral & John Connon School in South Mumbai. He studied at Imperial College London and was awarded a Bachelor of Engineering in Civil Engineering from the University of London in 1990. He later studied at the London Business School and in 1996 was awarded the International Executive Masters in Management from the University of London.

Career:

Mistry joined the family construction company, Shapoorji Pallonji & Co Ltd in 1991 as a director. Mistry was the Managing Director of Shapoorji Pallonji & Company, which is part of the Shapoorji Pallonji Group, and is also the Chairman of Tata Sons and Company. Tata Group.

In a 2013 article, **The Economist** classified him as "the most important industrialist in both India and the UK."

In 2018, his net worth was around $10 billion.

Tata Sons:

Mistry joined the board of Tata Sons on 1st September 2006, a year after his father's retirement. He served as Director of Tata Alexi Limited from 24th September 1990 to 26th October 2009 and was a Director of Tata Power Company Limited till 18th September 2006.

In 2013, Mistry was appointed as the chairman of Tata Sons. In addition, he was also the chairman of all major Tata companies including Tata Industries, Tata Steel, Tata Motors, Tata Consultancy Services, Tata Power, Tata Teleservices, Indian Hotels, Tata Global Beverages and Tata Chemicals.

The Tata Sons board voted on 24th October 2016 to remove Mistry from the chairmanship of Tata Sons.

2018 NCLT Verdict:

In July 2018, the **National Company Law Tribunal** (NCLT), which "addresses issues relating to Indian companies," issued a ruling in favor of Tata Sons over allegations of mismanagement leveled by Mistry, two months after the expulsion. On July 10th , Mistry said he would appeal against the decision.

2019 NCLAT Verdict:

In December 2019, the **National Company Law Appellate Tribunal** reinstated Mistry as chairman of Tata Sons for the remainder of his term, and declared that the appointment of TCS CEO Natarajan Chandrasekaran as executive chairman of Tata Sons was illegal. In January 2020, Tata Sons appealed to the Supreme Court against the NCLAT decision. Cyrus Mistry announced that he would not return to chair the group, but was interested in reserving his seat on the company's board. A three-judge bench of Chief Justice SA Bobde and Justices BR Gavai and Surya Kant, while hearing the appeal of Tata Sons on 10th January 2020, stayed the NCLAT order.

"We find that there are lapses in the judicial orders passed by the NCLAT," the bench said.

The Supreme Court of India also ordered that Tata Sons shall not exercise power under Article 25 of the Companies Act to exclude shares of minority holders in the company.

Personal life:

Mistry was married to Rohika Chagla, daughter of lawyer Iqbal Chagla and granddaughter of jurist MC Chagla. Iqbal Chagla has drawn up a strategy of action for Cyrus Mistry in the legal battle against Tata Sons.

The couple has two sons, Firoz Mistry and Jahan Mistry.

Mistry was an Irish citizen and a permanent resident of India (acquired Overseas Citizenship of India). According to a news published in the Irish newspaper, **The Independent,** Mistry sees himself as a global citizen.

His father, Pallonji Mistry passed away on 28th June 2022.

Death:

On 4th September 2022, Mistry and three members of the Pandole family visited Iranshah Atash Behram in Udvada. As confirmed by the Parsi High Priest, Khurshid Dastur, the group came to offer prayers after the deaths of Dinshaw Pandole and Pallonji Mistry.

While returning to Mumbai from Udvada, the Mercedes-Benz GLC in which they were traveling crashed at a speed of 90 km/h on a bridge over the Surya River near Charoti in Palghar on Ahmedabad-Mumbai, National Highway 8. District . Cyrus Mistry and Jehangir Pandole, who were seated in the back seat without wearing seat belts, were killed immediately after colliding with the rear of the front seats of the car. Mistry suffered severe head injuries as well as multiple fractures in the chest, head region, thigh and neck. Mistry and Pandole died due to multiple injuries to vital organs. The driver, Dr. Anahita Pandole, and her husband Darius Pandole, in the front row passenger seat, were wearing seat belts and survived injuries.

Investigation:

A seven-member forensic investigation team investigated the cause of the accident and concluded that the car accident was caused by a "faulty design" of the bridge and that the occupants had died because they were not wearing seat belts. The team member said, "We have concluded that there was an infrastructure issue which led to the accident. The parapet wall of the bridge was found to protrude into the shoulder lane. The design is found to be faulty." The three-lane road was suddenly L-shaped. Turned into a two-lane road with concrete dividers. The concrete divider was up to knee height and was not painted appropriately. There is a lack of warning at the scene and in the past several accidents have taken place at the same place. Mistry's car collided with a divider at a site with faulty road design. His death sparked a debate over inconsistent road design and seatbelt wear by rear seat passengers. The central government announced that it will start penalizing rear seat passengers with a fine of ₹1000 for not wearing a seat belt.

Tata Sons vs Cyrus Mistry:

In one of the most dramatic developments in recent times, the Tata Group's board of directors voted on 24th October 2016 to remove its chairman Cyrus Mistry with immediate effect and make Ratan Tata interim chairman, and in February 2017 to replace Mistry with Tata removed from the post of Director of Sons. The National Company Law Appellate Tribunal (NCLAT) had decided in December 2019 that the removal of Cyrus Mistry as chairman of Tata Sons was illegal and he should be reinstated. The Supreme Court of India is hearing the group's appeal for $111 billion to set aside an NCLAT order that had directed the Tata Group to reappoint the man it had fired as chairman. Ratan Tata is personally leading the charge in the case, and filed a separate petition challenging the verdict in the Supreme Court. The Supreme Court has stayed the NCLAT order that allowed the reinstatement of Cyrus Mistry as the chairman of Tata Sons in January 2020. However, the Supreme Court upheld the dismissal of Cyrus Mistry.

Shantanu Naidu

At the age of 28, Shantanu Naidu has achieved a position in the business industry which always remains a dream for many. According to reports, Shantanu Naidu gives Ratan Tata business tips for investing in start-ups.

Shantanu Naidu was born in 1993 in Pune Maharashtra. He is a renowned Indian Businessman, Engineer, Junior Assistant, DGM, Social Media Influencer, Writer and Entrepreneur. Shantanu Naidu is quite popular across the country as the Deputy General Manager of Tata Trusts.

Shantanu Naidu, an MBA from Cornell University, is the fifth generation of his family to work in the Tata Group.

According to his LinkedIn profile, Shantanu has been working in Tata Trusts since June 2017. Apart from this, Naidu has also worked as a Design Engineer in Tata Alexei.

Beginning your journey at Tata:

The youngster's dream came true when Ratan Tata invited him for a meeting after his Facebook post where he wrote about dog collars made with reflectors for stray dogs so that drivers can see them on the streets of Mumbai .

Shantanu Naidu wrote in his post, "The word spread and our work was published in the Tata newsletter."

Being a student organization, the funds were not enough to make these collars. So, he decided to use denim pants as the base material for making the collar. He collected denim pants from different houses and made 500 reflective collars in Pune and collared 500 dogs.

Wearing these collars made by him, the drivers could see the dogs from a distance even at night without street lights and hence the lives of the street dogs could be saved. His work was noted by many and his posts began to receive anonymous online comments about how the collar helped dogs become visible and eventually slowed down people.

Soon Naidu's work gained widespread attention and was highlighted in the Tata Company's newspaper, which received an invitation from Ratan Tata, the former Tata Group chairman and an animal activist, to Mumbai himself.

In 2016, Shantanu Naidu went to Cornell University in the US to pursue an MBA. When he completed his degree and returned in 2018, he joined Tata Trusts as Deputy General Manager in the Chairman's Office.

Shantanu won Ratan Tata's heart with his work:

Veteran businessman Ratan Tata is also a fan of Shantanu's good ideas. According to several reports, Shantanu Naidu helps Ratan Tata in his private investment start-up. Shantanu has won the heart of Ratan Tata with his work.

Interestingly, Ratan Tata has a strong belief in the country's start-up system and this may be the reason why start-ups that get Ratan Tata's backing often see a significant increase in their value.

An act of kindness:

Shantanu Naidu has his own Instagram handle **'On Your Sparks'**, through which he inspires students across the country who were afraid to enter the field of entrepreneurship. Amid the COVID-19 lockdown, Shantanu Naidu started an online conversation - 'On Your Sparks' - to help aspiring entrepreneurs. He started it based on his life lessons and turned them into entrepreneurial lessons. Now, he goes live on his Instagram account every Sunday with 'On Your Sparks' and charges Rs 500 for each participant and the funds go to **Motopaws** to help Street Dogs. Today, Motopaws has spread to over 20 cities and 4 countries.

A book on his life with Ratan Tata:

Not only this, Shantanu Naidu also authored a book titled '**I Come Upon a Lighthouse**', which is a small mirror of his life with business tycoon Ratan Tata.

Young Shantanu Naidu has carved a niche for himself in the business industry at a very young age and veteran business tycoon Ratan Tata is one of his admirers. Shantanu Naidu began his inspiring journey with an initiative to help street dogs and soon his hard work and dedication paved the way for who he is today. His journey is truly an inspiration for who we can become tomorrow.

Entity

Tata Consultancy Services:

Tata Consultancy Services was established in the year 1968. It started as a division of the Tata Group under the name "Tata Computer Centre.". Its main business then was to provide computer services to other companies in its own group. Soon the capabilities of computerization and computer services began to grow, and Fakir Chand Kohli, an electrical engineer at the Tata Electric Company, was made general manager of the "Tata Computer Centre". Shortly after, the company was renamed as Tata Consultancy Services.

TCS began its first software export project in 1974 when the company changed the hospital information system from Burhose Medium Systems COBOL to Burroughs Small Systems COBOL. This project is fully funded by ICL at TCS Mumbai.In 1980, TCS and one of its affiliates contributed 63% of the total exports of the Indian software industry, while the share of other companies was only $ 400 million. In 1984, TCS established its office in Santacruz Electronics Export Processing Zone, Mumbai.

TCS's business grew tremendously in the 1990s, as a result of which the company recruited on a large scale. In the early mid-1990s, TCS re-established itself as a software product manufacturer. In the late 1990s, TCS used a three-pronged strategy - developing new products that made more money, capturing domestic and other rapidly growing markets, and growing its size through mergers and acquisitions with other companies. In late 1998, the company decided to focus on new opportunities to make money, including Wi-K and Euro conversion. The company paid special attention to e-business in the late 1990s.

TCS became a publicly listed company in 2004.

On 8th October 2020, Tata Consultancy Services surpassed **Accenture** in market capitalization to become the world's most valuable IT company with a market cap of $144.73 billion. On 25th January 2021, Tata Consultancy Services again surpassed, Accenture by market capitalization, becoming the world's most valuable IT company with a market cap of $170 billion. On the same day, Tata Consultancy Services became India's most valuable company , which overtook Reliance Industries with a market cap of ₹ 12.55 lakh crore.

Office and Development Center

Indian Branches :

TCS's development centers and/or regional offices are located in the following Indian cities: Ahmedabad, Bangalore, Vadodara, Bhubaneswar, Chennai, Coimbatore, Delhi, Gandhinagar, Goa, Gurgaon, Hyderabad, Jamshedpur, Kochi, Kolkata, Lucknow, Mumbai, Noida, Pune and Thiruvananthapuram

Global Entities:

Africa: South Africa

Asia (outside India): Bahrain, China, Indonesia, Israel, Japan, Malaysia, Saudi Arabia, Singapore, South Korea, Taiwan, Thailand, UAE

Australia: Australia

Europe: Belgium, Denmark, Finland, France, Germany, Hungary, Iceland, Ireland, Italy, Luxembourg, Netherlands, Norway, Portugal, Spain, Sweden, Switzerland, United Kingdom

North America: Canada, Mexico, United States of America

South America: Argentina, Brazil, Chile, Colombia, Ecuador, Uruguay

TCS has established its Nearshore Centers in North America, Europe and Asia Pacific, Regional Development Centers in Hungary, Uruguay and Brazil, and a Global Development Center in China as well as in India.

In 2006, Tata acquired Comicrom SA of Chile. Financial Network Services Pvt Ltd of Australia, and Indian IT Resources AB of Sweden, are subsidiaries of TCS.

The company has established two subsidiaries: **TCS FNS PRIVATE LIMITED AUSTRALIA** and **DILIGENTA LIMITED UK**. The company has also established other subsidiaries such as Portugal Unipessol Limitada in

Portugal, Tata Consultancy Services Luxembourg SA in Luxembourg and Tata Consultancy Services Chile Limited, Chile. The company had 490 subsidiaries as on 31st March 2006.

In March 2006, the company acquired some of the businesses of **Pearl Group Services Limited** through its subsidiary **Diligenta Limited**. Included in this acquisition were certain insurance contracts and claims administration business and assets, including credit and technical know-how.

The company has entered into a joint venture by entering into an agreement with **Internet Global Services Limited**. TCS is joining hands with SEDS for GM deal, to get some part of the business.

In February 2007, TCS started a venture in China with Microsoft and three Chinese companies - Tata Information Technology (Shanghai) Company Limited.

Taj Group of Hotels:

Jamsetji Nusserwanji Tata, the founder of the Tata Group, inaugurated a grand hotel on the shores of the Arabian Sea in Mumbai (formerly known as Bombay) by the name of the Taj Mahal Palace on 16th December 1903. It was the first asset and first hotel of the Taj Group. There are many legends related to the hidden reasons behind the construction of this hotel by Jamsetji. According to one story, the reason behind this was his denial of entry to the Watson's Hotel in Mumbai (where only Europeans were allowed to go) due to racial discrimination.

In 1984, the Taj Group acquired, under a license agreement, the Taj Connemara in Chennai (now by Vivanta Taj - Connemara) and the Savoy Hotel in Ooty, with the opening of the Taj West End in Bangalore. |

In those days it was common in British India to allow only Europeans to enter hotels, but it seemed a bit awkward for a businessman of the same ability as Jamsetji Tata to build a hotel on this basis alone. In another story, he decided to open a hotel when a friend of his complained that there was no hotel of any kind in Bombay. But the most likely reason in this context is Lovett Fraser - Jamsetji's close friend and I.H.C.L. One of the first directors of the group - Kay, who says that this idea was going on in Jamsetji's mind for a long time and he had done extensive research on the subject.

He had no desire to own a hotel and just wanted to attract people to India and make Bombay better. Jamsetji is said to have traveled to London, Paris, Berlin and Dusseldorf to collect the interiors, artifacts and furniture of this hotel.

From the year 2000 onwards, the Taj Group started dividing its hotels and resorts into several sections under a business segregation policy.

Taj/Taj Luxury:- It is the luxury brand of Taj with the old Taj Hotels and Palaces. These hotels are built on commercial towns, historical sites, palaces, resorts and forest sites. Most of Taj's oldest and most famous hotels come under this brand.

Taj Exotica - Resorts and Spa Brand of Taj Group

Taj Safaris - Lodges made in various national parks and forest sanctuaries of India come under this brand. The brand is based on the concept of sustainable eco-tourism.

Vivanta by Taj - Vivanta by Taj Group is a contemporary luxury brand. These hotels are meant for the high purchasing power segment and are only marginally inferior to Taj Hotels in terms of luxury. Vivanta Hotels have come up at all commercial and tourist destinations,

The Gateway Hotels & Resorts - The brand is aimed at people with middle purchasing power and is considered a step down from Vivanta in the order of preference. Like Vivanta, all of them are located at commercial and tourist destinations.

TISCO Tata Iron and Steel Company:

Tata Iron and Steel Company (TISCO) was founded by Jamsetji Nusserwanji Tata and was established on 26th August 1907 by Sir Dorabji Tata. TISCO began production of pig iron in 1911 and steel in 1912 as an offshoot of Jamsetji's Tata Group. The first steel plant was built on 16th February 1912. During the First World War (1914–1918), the company made rapid progress.

In 1920, the Tata Iron and Steel Company incorporated **The Tinplate Company of India Limited (TCIL)** as a joint venture with the then Burma Shell to manufacture tinplates. TCIL is now Tata Tinplate and has a 70% market share in India.

Until 1939, it operated the largest steel plant in the British empire. The company began a major modernization and expansion program in 1951.

Later, in 1958, the program was upgraded to a 2 Million Metric Tonnes Per Annum (MTPA) project. By 1970, the company employed about 40,000 people in Jamshedpur, and 20,000 in neighboring coal mines.

Tata Steel was the highest profit making company of the Tata Group in November 2021.

Nationalization Efforts:

There were two attempts, one in 1971 and the other in 1979, when the company was nationalized. Both were unsuccessful attempts. In 1971, Indira Gandhi's regime tried to nationalize the company, but failed. In 1979, the Janata Party regime (1977–79), wanted to nationalize TISCO (now Tata Steel). At the behest of Biju Patnaik, the then Industries Minister George Fernandes, the Steel Minister threatened nationalization, but the move failed due to protests by unions.

In 1990, the company began to expand and established its subsidiary Tata Inc. in New York. The company changed its name from **TISCO** to **Tata Steel Limited** in 2005.

Formerly known as Tata Iron and Steel Company Limited (TISCO), Tata Steel is one of the top steel producing companies in the world with an annual crude steel capacity of 34 million tonnes. It is one of the world's most geographically diverse steel producers with operations and commercial presence around the world. The Group (excluding SEA operations) recorded a consolidated turnover of US$ 19.7 billion for the financial year ended on 31st March 2020. It is the second largest steel company (as measured by domestic production) in India after Steel Authority with an annual capacity of 13 million tonnes. Along with Tata Steel, SAIL and Jindal Steel and Power, there are only 3 Indian steel companies that have captive iron-ore mines, giving a price advantage to the three companies.

The Key Managerial Personnel (KMP) in Tata Steel Limited India is Kaushik Chatterjee as CFO (KMP) and Parvatisam Kanchinadham as Company Secretary. Kaushik Chatterjee, Mallika Srinivasan, Chandrasekaran Natarajan and 7 other members are currently attached as Directors.

Tata Steel operates in 26 countries with major operations in India, the Netherlands and the United Kingdom and employs approximately 80,500 people. Its largest plant (10 MTPA capacity) is located at Jamshedpur, Jharkhand. In 2007, Tata Steel acquired UK-based steel maker Corus.

In 2014 it was ranked 486th in the **Fortune Global 500** ranking of the world's largest corporations. It was the seventh most valuable Indian brand of 2013 according to Brand Finance.

In July 2019, Tata Steel Kalinganagar (TSK) was included in the list of Global Lighthouse Network of the World Economic Forum (WEF).

Tata Steel has been recognized as one of **India's Best Workplaces in Manufacturing**. This recognition has been received for the fifth time, highlighting the company's continued focus on fostering a culture of high-trust, integrity, growth and care for employees. Tata Steel has also been inclusive for its LGBTQ employees and also provides health insurance benefits for its LGBTQ employees' partners under the new HR policy.

Tata Steel has traditionally played an important role in the development of sports in India. He has been involved in the establishment of Tata Football Academy, TSAF Climbing Academy, Tata Archery Academy, Naval Tata Hockey Academy - Jamshedpur and Odisha Navy Tata Hockey High Performance Centre.

Acquisitions:

NatSteel in 2004: Tata Steel agreed to acquire the steelmaking operations of Singapore-based NatSteel for $486.4 million in cash. NatSteel ended 2003 with a turnover of $1.4 billion and profit before tax of $47 million. NatSteel's steel business will be carried on by the Company through a wholly owned subsidiary named NatSteel Asia Pte Ltd. The acquisition was completed in February 2005. At the time of the acquisition, NatSteel had a capacity of approximately 2 million tonnes per year of finished steel.

Millennium Steel in 2005: Tata Steel acquired a majority stake in Thailand-based steelmaker Millennium Steel for a total cost of $130 million. It paid Siam Cement US$73 million for a 40% stake and offered to pay 1.13 baht per share for another 25% of the shares held by other shareholders. Millennium Steel is now renamed as Tata Steel Thailand and is headquartered in Bangkok. On 31st March 2013, it held approximately 68% shares in the acquired company.

Corus in 2006: Tata Steel signed an agreement with the Anglo-Dutch company, Corus, to buy a 100% stake for £4.3 billion ($8.1 billion) at 455 pence per share. On 19th November 2006, the Brazilian steel company Companhia Sidergica Nacional (CSN) launched a counteroffer for Corus at 475 pence per share, valued at £4.5 billion. On 11th December 2006,

Tata increased its offer to 500 pence per share, a deal valued at £4.9 billion from CSN's offer of 515 pence per share. Corus' board immediately recommended both revised proposals to its shareholders. On 31st January 2007, Tata Steel won its bid for Corus after offering 608 pence per share, valuing Corus at £6.7 billion ($12 billion).

In 2005, Corus employed approximately 47,300 people worldwide, including 24,000 in the UK. At the time of acquisition, Corus was four times larger than Tata Steel in terms of annual steel production. Corus was the 9th largest producer of steel in the world, while Tata Steel was ranked 56th. The acquisition made Tata Steel the world's 5th largest producer of steel.

Tayo Rolls in 2008: formerly Tata-Yodogawa Limited is a metal manufacturing and processing company headquartered in Jamshedpur, India. It was established in 1968 as a joint venture between Tata Steel and Japan-based Yodogawa Steels. In 2008, the company made a rights issue, which was subscribed for about 50% of its total value - Rs 60-crore. Due to low membership, they were taken over by the promoters, resulting in Tayo Rolls becoming a subsidiary of Tata Steel. Tata Steel holds a 55.24% stake in Taio Rolls.

Steel Engineering and Vinosteel in 2007: Tata Steel through its wholly owned Singapore subsidiary, Natsteel Asia Pte Ltd, acquired controlling stake in both rolling mill companies based in Vietnam: Structure Steel Engineering Pte Ltd (100% stake) and Vinosteel Ltd (70% stake). The enterprise value for the acquisition was $41 million. With this acquisition, Tata Steel took over two rolling mills, the 250,000 ton per annum bar/wire rod mill operated by SSE Steel Ltd. and the 180,000 ton per annum strong bar mill operated by Winosteel Ltd.

Bhushan Steel in 2018: Tata Steel acquired the entire company in 2017-18, when insolvency proceedings were initiated against the former company on 26th July 2017 under IBC. Tata Steel emerged as the highest bidder and acquired the company through its wholly-owned subsidiary, Bamnipal Steel Limited. The name of the company was changed to Tata Steel BSL. Later in 2021, Tata Steel merged Bamnipal Steel Limited and Tata Steel BSL, making the latter a direct subsidiary of Tata Steel (72.65%).

Neelachala Ispat Nigam Limited in 2022: Tata Steel acquired a controlling stake in NINL through its wholly owned subsidiary, Tata Steel Long Products (TSLP). It acquired Odisha-based Neelachal Ispat Nigam

Limited (NINL) for Rs 12,100 crore (US$ 1.5 billion), beating Jindal Steel and JSW Steel.

Tata Motors:

Tata Motors was established in 1945 as a locomotive manufacturer. The Tata group entered the commercial vehicle sector in 1954 after forming a joint venture with Daimler-Benz of Germany. After years of dominating the commercial vehicle market in India, Tata Motors entered the passenger vehicle market in 1991 by launching the Tata Sierra, a sports utility vehicle based on the Tata mobile platform. Tata later launched the Tata Estate (1992; a station wagon design based on the earlier Tata Mobile), the Tata Sumo (1994, a 5-door SUV) and the Tata Safari.

Tata launched the **Indica** in 1998, a fully indigenous Indian passenger car, designed to suit the needs of Indian consumers, though styled by Idea, Italy. Although initially criticized by auto analysts, its excellent fuel economy, powerful engine and aggressive marketing strategy made it one of the best-selling cars in the history of the Indian automobile industry. A new version of the car, codenamed the **Indica V2**, was a major improvement over the previous version and quickly became a massive favourite. Tata Motors also successfully exported a large number of cars to South Africa. The success of Indica played an important role in the growth of Tata Motors.

In 2004, Tata Motors acquired Daewoo's South Korea-based truck manufacturing arm, Daewoo Commercial Vehicle Company, which was later renamed **Tata Daewoo.**

On 27th September 2004, Ratan Tata, chairman of Tata Motors, rang the opening bell at the New York Stock Exchange to mark the listing of Tata Motors.

In 2005, Tata Motors acquired a 21% controlling stake in Spanish bus and coach manufacturer Hispano Carrosera. Tata Motors continued to expand its market segment through the introduction of new products such as buses (developed jointly with Starbus and Globus, subsidiary Hispano Carrosera) and trucks (Novus, jointly developed with subsidiary Tata Daewoo).

In 2006, Tata formed a joint venture with Brazil-based Marcopolo, **Tata Marcopolo Bus**, to manufacture fully built buses and coaches.

In 2008, Tata Motors acquired English carmaker **Jaguar Land Rover,** maker of Jaguar and Land Rover, from Ford Motor Company.

In April 2022, the **Tata Avinya concept**: a new paradigm of innovation;

Tata acquired full ownership of **Hispano Carrosera** in 2009.

In 2009, its Lucknow plant was awarded the "Best" Rajiv Gandhi National Quality Award.

In 2010, Tata Motors acquired an 80% stake in Italian design and engineering company Trilix for €1.85 million. The acquisition is part of the company's plans to enhance its styling and design capabilities.

In 2012, Tata Motors announced that it would invest approximately ₹6 billion in the development of futuristic infantry combat vehicles in collaboration with DRDO.

In 2013, Tata Motors announced that it would sell in India, the world's first vehicle to run on compressed air (engines designed by the French company MDI) and dubbed the "Mini Cat".

In 2014, Tata Motors launched the **"T1 Prima Truck Racing Championship"** the first truck racing championship in India.

On 26th January 2014, Managing Director Carl Slim was found dead. He fell from the 22nd floor on the fourth floor of the Shangri-La Hotel in Bangkok, where he was to attend a Tata Motors Thailand meeting.

On 2nd November 2015, Tata Motors announced Lionel Messi as its global brand ambassador in New Delhi to promote and support passenger vehicles globally.

On 27th December 2016, Tata Motors announced Bollywood actor Akshay Kumar as the brand ambassador for its commercial vehicles range.

On 8th March 2017, Tata Motors announced that it has signed a 'Memorandum of Understanding' with **Volkswagen** to develop vehicles for India's domestic market.

On 3rd May 2018, Tata Motors announced that it sold its aerospace and defense business to another Tata Group entity, **Tata Advanced Systems,** to unlock its full potential.

On 29th April 2019, Tata Motors announced a partnership with Nirma University in Ahmedabad to offer B.Tech. degree program for the employees of its Sanand plant.

On 24th March 2020, Tata Motors Limited announced that it would wind up its passenger vehicles arm as a separate entity within the company.

On 5th March 2021, the shareholders of Tata Motors approved the winding up of its passenger vehicles business into a separate entity.

In August 2021, the company plans to recognize the efforts by gifting the Altroz hatchback, as a complimentary prize to the Indian Olympians who finished fourth at the Tokyo Olympics 2021 and missed out on a place for the bronze.

On 23rd August 2021, Tata Motors announced that it will launch its mini SUV Punch in the ongoing festive season.

On 30th May 2022, Tata Motors announced that it has signed an agreement to acquire a Ford India manufacturing plant in Sanand, Gujarat. Tata Motors agreed to pay 7.26 billion rupees ($91.5 million) for the manufacturing plant.

Tata Motors has vehicle assembly operations in India, the United Kingdom, South Korea, Thailand, Spain and South Africa. It plans to set up plants in Turkey, Indonesia and Eastern Europe.

Tata Motors Cars is a division of Tata Motors that produces passenger cars under the Tata Motors marque. Tata Motors is one of the top four passenger vehicle brands in India with products in the compact, midsize car and utility vehicle segments. The company's manufacturing base in India is spread over Jamshedpur (Jharkhand), Pune (Maharashtra), Lucknow (Uttar Pradesh), Pantnagar (Uttarakhand), Dharwad (Karnataka) and Sanand (Gujarat). Tata's dealership, sales, service and spare parts network includes over 3,500 touchpoints. Tata Motors has over 250 dealerships in over 195 cities across 27 states and four union territories in India. It has the third largest sales and service network after Maruti Suzuki and Hyundai.

Tata also has franchise/joint venture assembly operations in Kenya, Bangladesh, Ukraine, Russia and Senegal. Tata has dealerships in 26 countries across 4 continents. Tata is present in many countries, it has managed to create a large consumer base in the Indian subcontinent, such as India, Bangladesh, Bhutan, Sri Lanka and Nepal.

Tata Daewoo (officially Tata Daewoo Commercial Vehicle Company and formerly Daewoo Commercial Vehicle Company) is a commercial vehicle manufacturer headquartered in Gunsan, Jeollabuk-do, South Korea, and a wholly owned subsidiary of Tata Motors. It is the second largest heavy commercial vehicle manufacturer in South Korea and was acquired by Tata Motors in 2004. The major reason behind the acquisition was to reduce Tata's dependence on the Indian commercial vehicle market (which accounted for around 94% of its sales in the MHCV segment and around 84% in the light commercial vehicle segment) and heavy-tonne. Expand your product portfolio by leveraging Daewoo's strengths in the load segment.

Tata Motors has worked with Tata Daewoo to develop trucks such as Novus and World Trucks and buses including **Globebus** and **Starbus**. In 2012, Tata began developing a new line to manufacture competitive and fuel-efficient commercial vehicles to face the competition generated by the entry of international brands such as Mercedes-Benz, Volvo and Navistar in the Indian market.

Jaguar Land Rover:

Jaguar Land Rover is a British premium automaker headquartered in Whitley, Coventry, United Kingdom, and has been a wholly-owned subsidiary of Tata Motors since June 2008, when it was acquired from Ford Motor Company of the USA. Its principal activity is the development, manufacture and sale of Jaguar luxury and sports cars and Land Rover premium four-wheel-drive vehicles.

Jaguar Land Rover has two design centers and three assembly plants in the United Kingdom. Under Tata's ownership, Jaguar Land Rover has launched new vehicles including the Range Rover Evoque, Jaguar F-Type, Jaguar XE, Jaguar XJ (X351), the second generation Range Rover Sport, and the Jaguar XF, the fourth generation Land. Rover Discovery, Range Rover Velar and Range Rover (L405).

JD Power of the US rates Land Rover and Jaguar are the two worst brands for starting quality. The Jaguar F-Pace included Consumer Reports in its list of the 10 least reliable cars in February 2019. The editors cited "electronics, drive systems, power tools, noise and leaks" as problematic aspects.

The Jaguar Land Rover subsidiary was struggling as of 2019 and Tata Motors cut its investment in JLR by $3.9 billion. Much of the financial problem was due to a 50% drop in sales in China during 2019, although the situation was improving. Still, Tata was ready to consider a partnership with another company, according to a statement in mid-October as long as the partnership agreement would allow Tata to retain control of the business. The company ruled out any possibility of selling JLR to any other entity.

Tata Technologies:

Tata Technologies Limited (TTL) is a 43% owned subsidiary of Tata Motors that provides design, engineering and business process outsourcing services to the automotive industry. It is headquartered in the Hinjewadi business district of Pune and has operations in London, Detroit and Thailand. Its customers include Ford, General Motors, Honda and Toyota.

British engineering and design services company **Incat International,** specializing in engineering and design services and product lifecycle management in the automotive, aerospace and engineering sectors, is a wholly-owned subsidiary of TTL. It was acquired by TTL in August 2005 for ₹4 billion.

In 2017, TAL, a subsidiary of Tata Motors, built India's first industrial artificial robot for micro, small and medium enterprises.

European Technical Center:

Tata Motors European Technical Center (TMETC) is an automotive design, engineering and research company based at the Warwick Manufacturing Group (WMG) on the campus of the University of Warwick in England. It was established in 2005 and is a wholly-owned subsidiary of Tata Motors. It was the joint developer of World Trucks.

In September 2013, it was announced that a new national automotive innovation complex would be built at WMG in Warwick's main campus at a cost of £100 million. The initiative will be a partnership between Tata Motors, the university and Jaguar Land Rover, with £30 million in funding from Tata Motors.

Tata Marcopolo:

Tata Marcopolo is a bus-manufacturing joint venture between Tata Motors (51%) and Brazil-based Marcopolo SA (49%). The joint venture manufactures and assembles fully built buses and coaches, aiming to develop rapid transportation systems on a large scale. It harnesses technology and expertise in chassis and aggregates from Tata Motors, and information in processes and systems for bodybuilding and bus body design from Marcopolo. Tata Marcopolo has launched a low-floor city bus which is widely used by transport corporations in many Indian cities. Its manufacturing facilities are located in Dharwad, Karnataka State, India and Lucknow, India.

Tata Motors hopes to buy its partner Marcopolo's 49% stake in the bus-making joint venture for ₹100 crore by February 2021. Competition provision in India is for the same period.

Fiat-Tata:

Fiat-Tata is an India-based joint venture between Tata and Stelantis Fiat that produces Fiat and Tata branded passenger cars as well as engines and transmissions. Tata Motors has gained access to Fiat's diesel engine and transmission technology through a joint venture.

The two companies also previously had a distribution joint venture through which Fiat products were sold in India through joint Tata-Fiat dealerships. This distribution arrangement was terminated in March 2013; Fiat is distributed in India by Fiat Automobiles India Limited, a wholly -owned subsidiary of Fiat.

Tata Hitachi Construction Machinery:

Tata Hitachi Construction Machinery is a joint venture between Tata Motors and Hitachi that manufactures excavators and other construction equipment. It was earlier known as Telcon Construction Solutions.

Tata Motors European Technical Center:

Tata Motors European Technical Center is an automotive design, engineering and research company. It is based at Warwick Manufacturing Group (WMG) on the campus of the University of Warwick in the United Kingdom. It was established in 2005 and is a wholly-owned subsidiary of Tata Motors. It was the joint developer of World Trucks. In September 2013 it was announced that a new National Automotive Innovative Campus would be built at WMG in Warwick's main campus at a cost of £92 million. The initiative will be a partnership between Tata Motors, the university and Jaguar Land Rover, with £30 million in funding coming from Tata Motors.

Hyundai-Tata:

Tata Motors and Hyundai are in a joint venture to provide transmission for the Tata Harrier model.

Tata Nano:

Tata Nano is often cited as the cheapest car in the world. The Nano was launched in 2009 as a city car, with an aim to appeal as an affordable option to the segment of the Indian population that primarily owns motorcycles and has not bought their first car. Initially priced at ₹100,000 (US$1,500), the vehicle attracted much attention for its relatively low price tag. However, the Nano was rated very poorly for safety and in 2018, Tata Group Chairman Cyrus Mistry called the Tata Nano a failed project, with production ending in May 2018.

Tata Super Ace:

Tata Ace, India's first indigenously developed sub-one-ton minitruck, was launched in May 2005. The Minitruck was a huge success in India, with auto analysts claiming that the Ace has changed the dynamics of the light commercial vehicle (LCV) market in the country creating a new market segment called the small commercial vehicle segment. ACE rapidly emerged as the first choice for transporters and solo truck owners for city and rural transport.

Tata Prima:

The Tata Prima is a range of heavy trucks that were first introduced as the company's 'Global' trucks in 2008. Tata Prima was the winner of 'Commercial Vehicle of the Year' at the Apollo Commercial Vehicle Awards, 2010 and 2012.

The Tata Harrier is a 5-seater SUV that rivals the MG Hector and the Jeep Compass. The car uses Fiat's engine which is a 2.0L-4 cylinder turbocharged diesel motor and transmission from Hyundai which is a 6-speed, available in both manual and automatic. The Tata Harrier is derived from the H5X concept showcased at the 2018 Auto Expo. It was launched on 23rd January 2019.

The car is a C-segment crossover SUV based on the OmegaArc platform, which is essentially a re-engineered version of the Jaguar Land Rover D8 platform. A petrol variant of the Harrier is confirmed to be launched in 2022-23.Tata Harrier is also available in Nepal as H5.

Tata Memorial:

Tata Memorial Center is located in Parel, Mumbai (India). It is a center for cancer treatment and research. This institute is aided by the **Department of Atomic Energy** of India. TMC is a classic example of how well private and public cooperation can work together.

After Meherbai Tata died of blood cancer in 1932, her husband Dorabji Tata wanted to bring to India a facility similar to the hospital where his wife was treated. After Dorabji's death, his successor, Sir Nowroji Saklatwala, took the effort forward. Ultimately, as a result of JRD Tata's support, the dream of the Tata Memorial Hospital, a seven-storey building, in the heart of Parel, the labor area of Mumbai, was realized on 28th February 1941.

In 1957, the Ministry of Health of India temporarily took over the Tata Memorial Hospital. But JRD Tata and the pioneer of India's nuclear power program - Homi Jehangir Bhabha - were able to foresee the role of radiation in the process of cancer treatment, from imaging to staging and actual treatment. In 1962 the administrative control of the hospital was transferred to the Department of Atomic Energy (DAE) of India. After four years, the Cancer Research Institute and TMC, established in 1952, were merged.

Starting from an 80-bed hospital spread over an area of 15,000 square metres, TMC now covers an area of about 70,000 square meters with over 600 beds. In 1941, the annual budget of Rs. 5 lakh, he is now Rs. It has been close to 120 crores.

Today, TMC treats about a third of cancer patients in India. It is an important site on the global health map where 60% of first aid patients are treated free of cost.

The center places great emphasis on education in the field of cancer. More than 250 students, medical professionals, scientists and technicians are trained in the hospital. The Indian Department of Atomic Energy has set up a state-of-the-art R&D center named 'Advanced Center for Treatment and Education in Cancer' at Kharghar in Navi Mumbai to focus on research in cancers relevant to India and South Asia.

Some facts about Tata Memorial:

In 2008, some 52,000 patients were treated at TMC, about 65 per cent of them were treated free of cost. The center has 620 inpatient beds (98 percent full) and treats 140 patients daily.

TMC is supported by several cancer centers across India, among them Regional Cancer Centers at Ahmedabad, Thiruvananthapuram, Nagpur, Gwalior and Hyderabad, Civil Hospital, Shillong and Jorhat Hospital, Jorhat (Assam).

TMC has some 300 postgraduate and doctoral students and also has its own university. The center offers residential programs in General Surgery, Radiotherapy, Pathology and Anesthesiology, super specialty programs and research programs. Apart from this, it also conducts training courses of six to eighteen months duration and also conducts distance education courses.

The center operates collaborative initiatives with the **World Health Organization**, the **National Institutes of Health**, Washington DC (USA), IARC, **Lyon** (France) and the **Bill & Melinda Gates Foundation**.

In 2002, TMC established the Advanced Center for Treatment Education and Research in Cancer (ACTREC) at Kharghar, Navi Mumbai. Spread over 60 acres in the Satellite city of Mumbai, ACTREC has a Clinical Research Center and a Cancer Research Centre.

Tata Powers:

Tata Powers is a company of the Tata family engaged in the generation, transmission and distribution of electricity in the private sector. It was already working in the field of power distribution, but it has ambitious plans to expand in the field of power generation. After the experimental generation of electricity at Jojobeda adjoining Chhotagovindpur in Jamshedpur, in the first phase, new units are being set up at Maithon in Dhanbad, Munra in Gujarat and Cuttack (Narjamathapur) in Orissa.

Tata Capital:

Tata Capital, a subsidiary of Tata Sons Limited, was established in the year 2007. It is the financial services arm of the USD 108 billion Tata Group. It is the holding company of Tata Capital Financial Services Limited (TCFSL), Tata Securities Limited and Tata Capital Housing Finance Limited.

The Company is registered with Reserve Bank of India (RBI) as a Systemically Important Deposit taking Non-Banking Financial Company. Tata Capital provides services such as commercial finance, investment banking, consumer loans, private equity, treasury advisory and credit cards. It serves corporate, retail and institutional clients through its wholly-owned subsidiary, TCFSL.

Tata Chemicals:

Tata Chemicals Limited is an Indian global company headquartered in Mumbai, India, in chemicals, crop protection and specialty chemistry products. The company is one of the largest chemical companies in India with operations in India, Europe, North America and Africa. Tata Chemicals is a subsidiary of the Tata Group group. Tata Chemicals has a publicly listed subsidiary called Rallis India.

Tata Chemicals has the second largest soda ash production capacity plant in India. This was the second soda ash plant built in India by Kapil Ram Vakil (grandson of late Indian Justice Nanabhai Haridas), which started functioning in the year 1944. The township Mithapur, derives its name from "Mitha", which means salt in the Gujarati language. ,

Since 2006, Tata Chemicals has owned Brunner Mond, a chemical company in the United Kingdom with operations in Magadi (Kenya) and General Chemicals in the United States.

On 27th March 2008, Tata Chemicals Limited acquired 100 percent, with all these acquisitions increasing the combined capacity of production to approximately 5.17 million tonnes of soda ash.

In April 2010, Tata Chemicals acquired a 25% stake in the ammonia-urea fertilizer complex in Gabon for US$290 million. The first phase of the plant will have full operating capacity of 2.2 billion tonnes of ammonia and 3.85 billion tonnes of urea per day.

In 2019, the Tata Group transferred the branded food business of Tata Chemicals to Tata Global Beverages (now Tata Consumer Products) in an all-share deal.

In 2016, Tata Chemicals sold its urea business to Pune-based Yara India, which is part of Norwegian chemical company Yara International.

In 2022, Tata Chemicals through its subsidiary, Tata Chemicals Europe, set up the UK's first industrial-scale carbon capture and utilization plant. The plant can capture 40,000 tonnes of carbon dioxide per year.

The Tata Chemicals Innovation Center, a research and development center located in Pune, Maharashtra, started operations in 2004. The team of scientists is working in the following areas: Food Science and Technology, Advanced Materials, Green Chemistry, Biochemistry, Metabolites and Nutraceuticals. Other innovation centers include

Rallis Innovation Chemistry Hub (RICH) and Metahelix Life Sciences in Bengaluru and Tata Chemicals R&D Center in Mithapur, Gujarat.

Tata Communications:

Tata Communications Limited is an Indian telecommunications company formerly known as Videsh Sanchar Nigam Limited (VSNL). It was earlier a state-owned telecommunications service provider and was owned by the Department of Telecommunications, Ministry of Communications, Government of India. It was sold by the Department of Telecommunications, Ministry of Communications, Government of India to the Tata Group when the Atal Bihari Vajpayee-Bharatiya Janata Party-National Democratic Alliance was in power. Presently the company is part of the Tata Group.

Tata's communications network spans over 500,000 kilometers (310,000 mi) of subsea fiber and over 210,000 kilometers (130,000 mi) of terrestrial fiber. The company has invested $1.19 billion in its global subsea fiber network. It provides network services and software-defined network platforms such as Ethernet, SD-WAN, Content Delivery Network (CDN), Internet, multiprotocol label switching (MPLS), and private lines. It has a data center, cloud (private cloud and public cloud management) with over 400 presences (POPs) and co-location across 44 sites.

It is listed on Bombay Stock Exchange and National Stock Exchange of India. It also has stakes in its Sri Lankan subsidiaries, Tata Communications Lanka.

The company is listed as one of AON Hewitt's Best Employers in India for 2017.

The business was established in 1986 as Videsh Sanchar Nigam Limited (VSNL). Under the chairmanship of BK Singal (1991–1998), VSNL launched the first publicly available internet scheme in India in 1995. The international arm of VSNL (VSNL International) was started in 2004, after the Government of India started disinvestment of public sector units in India. VSNL was completely acquired by the Tata Group and was renamed as Tata Communications on 13th February.

In 2009, Tata Communications and Tyco Telecommunications completed the TGN-Intra Asia cable system.

In 2012, the company completed its network across Egypt connecting Europe with India. This created a sub-fiber network that travels around the world. The 9,280-kilometre (5,770 mi) Eurasian section of the Tata Global Network runs across the Mediterranean Sea and the Middle East, connecting Mumbai with Marseille. as well as providing low-latency connections with a round-trip delay of 92 ms and speeds between 2 Mbit/s and 10 Gbit/s.

The company has international bandwidth illumination capability in excess of 15 terabits per second.

In January 2016, Windstream Communications announced that it would be moving its 100 Gigabit Ethernet (100G) network from New Jersey data center operator NJFX's presence at Tata's Cable Landing Station (CLS) in Wall Township, New Jersey to the Internet of Ashburn, Virginia.

Tata Communications Transformation Services (TCTS), a 100% subsidiary of Tata Communications Limited, provides business transformation, managed network operations, network outsourcing and consulting services to telecommunications companies around the world.

Tata Communications Payment Solutions Limited (TCPSL), formerly known as Tata Communications Banking Infra Solutions, is a wholly-owned subsidiary of Tata Communications. TCPSL is one of the fastest growing payment solutions experts in India, offering end-to-end B2B and B2C solutions. Being a 100% Banking and Financial Services centric organization, TCPSL provides one stop payment solution to all categories of banks including PSU, Private, MNC and Co-operative banks. TCPSL's White Label ATM offering is foraying into the B2C segment under the Indicash brand name. With this it is the first white label ATM service provider in the country. Under this service offering, TCPSL provides ATM services across the country through Indicash ATM network with special focus on semi urban and rural areas.

Tanishq Jewellery:

Tanishq is an Indian jewellery brand and a division of Titan Company. Established in 1994, Tanishq is headquartered in Bangalore, Karnataka, India.

Tanishq was launched by **Titan Company** in the late 1980s. In the early 1990s, the India exchange issue was settled, and Titan Company chose to focus the brand on the Indian market. The first production plant was launched in August 1992 and Tanishq's first store opened in 1996. Tanishq was India's first jewelery retail brand.

The first years of Tanishq recorded consistent losses. In 2000, Managing Director Xerxes Desai selected Bhaskar Bhat as his successor. Starting in 2000, its net worth began to grow, and by 2003, Tanishq was one of the top 5 retailers in India, and Titan made up 40% of the company's revenue.

In the early 2000s, Tanishq opened stores internationally in the Middle East and the United States (Chicago and New Jersey), but closed them before the end of the decade.

Tanishq crowned the beauty pageant for Femina Miss India 2007. As of 2008, Tanishq had 105 stores in 71 cities in India. In 2011, the Tanishq Group launched a sub-brand called **Mia** for working women. In November 2012, Tanishq reached a milestone when it opened its 150th showroom in India.

In April 2014, the brand started exporting to the United Arab Emirates. In July 2014, Tanishq announced that it had discontinued its gold deposit schemes to comply with the **Companies Act 2013**, schemes that enable its customers to save to buy gold, but it was discontinued a few months later. It was launched back in a format that obeys the new laws.

As of June 2014, Tanishq had 167 retail stores across the country, and announced the opening of 30 more by the end of 2015.

In 2017, Tanishq launched a sub-brand called **Rivaah** targeting the marriage segment. In January 2017, the Titan Group merged its Gold Plus stores with the larger Tanishq retail brand. In April 2017, Tanishq launched the sub-brand **Miraya** to cater to women under 40. In December 2017, Tanishq launched its first line of products for men, the **Avir line.**

Titan:

Titan Company Limited is an Indian products company that mainly manufactures fashion accessories such as jewellery, watches and eyewear. A part of the Tata Group and started as a joint venture with **Tamil Nadu Industrial Development Corporation (TIDCO),** the company has its corporate headquarters in Electronic City, Bangalore, and registered office in Hosur, Tamil Nadu.

Titan Company started operations in 1984 under the name **Titan Watches Limited.** In 1994, Titan traded in jewelery with Tanishq and later in eyewear with **Titan EyePlus**. In 2005, it launched its youth fashion accessories brand **Fastrack.** The company is the largest branded jewelery manufacturer in India with over 80% of its total revenue coming from the jewelery segment. As of 2022, Titan has a 6% market share in India's jewelery market. As of 2019, it is also the fifth largest watch maker in the world. It is the most trusted Indian brand.

1984-1990:

Titan Company Limited was inaugurated on 26th July 1984 in Chennai under the name Titan Watches Limited. A plant for manufacturing Quartz Analog Electronic Watches was established at the Tamil Nadu State Industry Promotion Corporation, Industrial Area Limited at Hosur. In November 1986, Titan Company and Casio signed a **Memorandum of Understanding** on a proposal to manufacture 2 million digital and analog-digital watches. In 1989, a Satellite Case Plant was established at Dehradun, Uttarakhand with presently an annual production capacity of 500,000 watch cases.

1991-2000:

In September 1993, the company changed its name to Titan Industries Limited as it entered the category of products other than watches.

In 1994, Titan launched its jewelery brand, Tanishq.

In 1998, the company launched its watch and accessories brand, Fastrack, to compete with Timex, which was targeted at a younger audience.

2001-2010:

In 2001, Titan launched the children's watch brand **Dash**. The brand saw poor performance and was discontinued in 2003. In 2004, the company entered into an agreement with the Moet Hennessy Louis Vuitton Group to service the latter range of watches in India through its customer care centres. In 2005, Fastrack was established as an independent subsidiary brand with focus on urban youth. With an aim to become a fashion brand, Fastrack launched sunglasses in the same year and in 2009 launched bags, belts and wallets.

2011-Present:

Titan acquired Swiss watchmaker **Favre-Leuba** in 2011 to enter the European market. In 2013, Titan forayed into the fragrance segment with the skin brand and later that year, it forayed into the helmet category under its own brand Fastrack. In the same year, it changed its name to Titan Company Limited. In 2014, it entered into a joint venture with Montblanc to set up its retail stores in India.

In 2016, Titan opened prescription lens manufacturing facilities in Noida, Kolkata and Mumbai to improve its order processing times. In 2018, Titan merged its jewelery brand, **Gold Plus**, with Tanishq targeting customers in South India, to establish the brand's presence in the South.

Tanera is an ethnic wear brand from Titan that sells hand woven sarees from various weaving groups in India. The brand was launched in 2016. The first retail store was opened in Bengaluru in 2017, followed by more stores in New Delhi and Hyderabad.

In addition, Titan recently (during the last quarter of 2016) announced the soon-to-be-launched range of affordable smartwatches under its own brands like **Sonata and Fastrack.**

In 2016, Titan entered the wearables market by introducing its smartwatch, the **Juxt,** created in collaboration with Hewlett Packard. In 2017, the company launched a fitness tracker named Gesture Band under its youth accessories brand, Fastrack. In the same year, it invested $3 million in Cowell Tee, a Singapore-based wearables technology company. In 2018, the company added new fitness tracker bands. As of 2018, the company had a 7.4% market share in the wearable devices market.

In November 2020, Titan opened its first overseas Tanishq store in Dubai as well as an exclusive website for Dubai to showcase its collections.

As of 2022, Titan has a 6% market share in India's jewelery market.

Thoughts of Ratan Tata

1. "I don't believe in taking right decisions. I take decisions and then make them right."

2. "Business need to go beyond the interest of their companies to the communities they serve."

3. "People still believe what they read is necessarily the truth."

4. "If you want to walk fast, walk alone. But if you want to walk far, walk together."

5. "I have been constantly telling people to encourage people, to question the unquestioned and not to be ashamed to bring up new ideas, new processes to get things done."

6. "I've often felt that the Indian Tiger has not been unleashed."

7. "Ups and downs in life are very important to keep us going, because a straight line even in an ECG means we are not alive."

8. "If it stands the test of public scrutiny, do it... If it doesn't stand the test of public scrutiny then don't do it."

9. "Power and wealth are not two of my main stakes."

10. "None can destroy iron, but its own rust can! Likewise none can destroy a person, but its own mindset can!"

11. "Apart from values and ethics which I have tried to live by, the legacy I would like to leave behind is a very simple one – that I have always stood up for what I consider to be the right thing, and I have tried to be as fair and equitable as I could be."

12. "Don't be serious, enjoy life as it comes."

13. "I admire people who are very successful. But if that success has been achieved through too much ruthlessness, then I may admire that person, but I can't respect him."

14. "I have always been very confident and very upbeat about the future potential of India. I think it is a great country with great potential."

15. "There are many things that, if I have to relive, maybe I will do it another way. But I would not like to look back and think what I have not been able to."

THE END